IT'S A CAT'S WORLD...

you just live in it

ALSO BY JUSTINE A. LEE

It's a Dog's Life . . . but It's Your Carpet:
Everything You Ever Wanted to Know About Your
Four-Legged Friend

IT'S A CAT'S WORLD...

you just live in it

*Everything You Ever Wanted to
Know About Your Furry Feline*

JUSTINE A. LEE, DVM, DACVECC

THREE RIVERS PRESS
NEW YORK

Published in the United States by Three Rivers Press, an imprint of the Crown Publishing Group, a division of Random House, Inc., New York.

www.crownpublishing.com

Three Rivers Press and the Tugboat design are registered trademarks of Random House, Inc.

Some of the material in this book originally appeared in the author's previous work, *It's a Dog's Life . . . but It's Your Carpet* (Three Rivers Press, 2008).

LIBRARY OF CONGRESS CATALOGING-IN-PUBLICATION DATA

Lee, Justine A.
   It's a cat's world—you just live in it : everything you ever wanted to know about your furry feline / Justine Lee.
      p.   cm.
1. Cats—Miscellanea. I. Title.
SF445.5.L44 2008
636.8—dc22   2008027799

ISBN 978-0-307-39350-0

Printed in the United States of America

Design by Nora Rosansky

10 9 8 7 6 5 4 3 2 1

First Edition

May 2009

To Ma and Ba, for not making me go to med school . . .

To Seamus and Echo, the best cats *ever,* for de-stressing me every evening on the sofa by draping me in cat, and for teaching me that life should be spent relaxing and catnapping in a sunbeam . . .

CONTENTS

Chapter 2 **CURIOSITY KILLED THE CAT**

Chapter 3 FANCY FELINE

Chapter 4 KRAZY KITTY

Chapter 5 TRAINING THE FOUR-LEGGED BEAST

Chapter 6 CATKINS DIET

Chapter 7 **THE GREAT INDOORS**

Chapter 8 POISONING THE PUSSY

Chapter 9 SEX, DRUGS, AND ROCK AND ROLL

Chapter 10 THE VET AND THE PET

IT'S A CAT'S WORLD...

you just live in it

Chapter 1

CATS RULE AND DOGS DROOL

CATS are not small dogs, and any cat owner will kindly tell you that *cats rule and dogs drool*. At last count, there were 76 million cat owners compared to a measly 68 million dog owners in America, and for good reason. For all you apartment dwellers, cats are convenient—they don't take up a lot of room, they greet you and love you when you come home to that empty studio, they're lower maintenance, you can leave food out for them when you leave for the weekend, you don't have to walk them outside, and most important, they don't drool!

This chapter will guide the novice to experienced cat owner through the idiosyncrasies of owning these independent, aloof, but lovable creatures. Never owned a cat before? Don't get one without reading this chapter first, so you know all their lovable feline flaws. (Yes, they do *indeed* have a few, but don't we all?) On the other hand, maybe you've owned several cats for years, but still aren't sure why they do the crazy things they do. Find out exactly why your cat hisses, purrs, farts, and pukes. Get the answers to your perplexing questions on why cats are, plainly, just cats.

As a veterinarian, I obviously love both dogs and cats. But you'd be surprised—there are veterinarians out there who prefer just one species! If you take your kitty to an all-cat veterinary hospital, you can safely bet that your veterinarian prefers cats over dogs. My best friend, whom I love dearly (and want to be reincarnated as her next dog since she spoils them rotten), happens to be a veterinarian who dislikes cats. Don't get me wrong—she'll pet them and cuddle with them, but she just doesn't want to own one (or more specifically, she doesn't want to deal with a kitty litter box). So choose your veterinarian carefully (hint: you want a well-balanced one who loves *both* dogs and cats if you happen to have multiple pairs of four-legged friends at home). Personally, I spend more time with dogs because I like to romp around outdoors in the mud, but I still own and love cats. In fact, I've realized nothing is more stress relieving than coming home after a long day at work to relax on the sofa draped in cat.

My first official pet (as an adult) was a cat. I adopted Seamus, a gray and white male tabby, during my internship at Angell Memorial Animal Hospital in Boston. Seamus, a four-week-old kitten at that time, was brought into the ER after being "accidentally" stepped on. He was severely comatose, blind, and partially paralyzed, but after treating him for head trauma and brain swelling, he quickly improved a few days later. I was concerned that this was either a really unfortunate accident or a potential cat abuse case. While I'm grateful the original owners were humane enough to bring him in, they never came back to pick him up (guess they didn't want to pay their $273 bill), so I ended up adopting him. I like to think that Seamus has found a much better home since. I became his lucky new owner, and he became my "first feline love" from the whole experience.

One of the reasons I adopted Seamus (besides his vulnerable, adorable, and helpless state) was because I had never had a full-fledged pet. He was going to be my first "trial" pet, and as a freshly graduated veterinarian, I wanted to make sure that I truly could be a good animal owner too! Don't get me wrong—I had lots of cats and dogs growing up, but I had never, up to that point in my midtwenties, owned a pet as a "grown-up" (in other words, as a financially, mentally, and emotionally responsible adult, caring for another living creature). As a veterinarian, I purposely thought it was time to adopt a cat so I could understand the idiosyncrasies of cat ownership. I didn't know anything about the day-to-day life with a cat (aside from what I learned in veterinary school). I wanted to know about litter boxes, clay versus clumping options, behavioral problems, and general husbandry of cats (which doesn't mean that your husband takes care of them).

Since then, Seamus has grown on me like white on rice. As an "only child" (I can handle only so much responsibility at once, folks!), Seamus was very attached to me—in other words, he slept on my head. We had some feline housemates during my residency, so he had some kitty friends, but he lost his "only child" status shortly thereafter when I rescued JP, an eight-week-old pit bull. JP, named after Jamaica Plain, an up-and-coming (i.e., ghetto) area of Boston, was abandoned at the hospital with parvovirus. Apparently his owners couldn't afford to treat him either and surrendered him for lifesaving care. As a result, I became the lucky owner of yet another wonderful pet. JP and Seamus were instant brothers; they slept together, wrestled together, and romped around chasing each other. Once JP grew out of his puppy stage (i.e., grew to be fifty pounds), Seamus found that wrestling wasn't quite what it used to be. Thankfully, Seamus was appeased a few years later with a more feasibly sized feline friend when I adopted Echo, an all-black, juvenile male stray cat.

I first met Echo when I was performing routine veterinary exams at a local shelter. I instantly diagnosed him with a severe heart defect the minute I picked him up to examine him. Echo's heart murmur was so loud that it was vibrating through his chest wall and I could feel it when I scooped him up out of his cage. Unfortunately, he was born with this heart defect, and I was shocked that he had survived anesthesia for declawing and neutering prior to his arrival at the shelter. I adopted Echo knowing that he'd have a shortened life span, but I wanted to give him the best quality of life before he went into heart failure. So that's how Echo got his veterinary-geeky name: he was named after "echocardiogram," the technical term for a heart ultrasound (I foresaw a lot of these expensive procedures in his near, but short, future). Just to prove me wrong, Echo is still alive and kickin', despite my estimate that he'd only live a year or two (which is why veterinarians hate answering, "How long is he gonna live, Doc?"). Thankfully, all three of my pets get on grandly, and *I've* been the one who has been blessed by adopting these "rejects" that nobody else wanted.

Why do cats purr?

Why, oh why, does loud purring have to occur at 1 A.M. just when I fall asleep? Why can't my cat just purr at dinnertime or during evening TV-sofa time? Purring is that unusual vibration that is produced by nerve stimulation to the voice box muscles and the diaphragm (that sheet of muscle that separates your organs in your chest from your abdomen). The frequency and pattern of purring occurs between 25 and 150 hertz,[1] so it can be loud enough to wake you up when Max is sleeping on your head. Purring can occur during both inspiration and expiration and may look like your cat is breathing harder than usual. The cause and exact mechanism of purring still seem to elude even the smartest scientists and veterinarians (cats would be happy to tell you that they are smarter than humans). While purring doesn't seem to have any evolutionary purpose, I suspect that cats purr for the functional reason of bonding with their loved ones (i.e., you or their kittens). Cats mostly purr when they are comfortable and enjoying human contact, while mother cats may purr during nursing. The *rare* cat may purr when stressed or really sick (i.e., going to the veterinary clinic), so don't always interpret it as a sign of happiness.

Not sure if your cat is purring or having difficulty breathing? It's important to know the difference, especially if you are the owner of a cat with asthma or heart problems. When in doubt, double-check by putting your hand alongside your cat's chest. If you don't feel vibrations, your cat may have difficulty breathing, and this should prompt an immediate veterinary visit. If you do feel vibrations, and your cat looks content sleeping on your pillow after a nice Fancy Feast snack, then this is probably normal, I'm-happy-to-be-near-my-human purring. You should be flattered that your cat is satisfied in your presence.

Why do cats hiss?

It might just be a weird veterinary thing, but when I notice two work colleagues arguing in front of me, sometimes I hiss at them. It's my animal way of communicating to them that they're fighting like cats and are being, well, kind of catty. I guess non-animal people would think that's really weird. That said, why do cats hiss?

Cats hiss to sound intimidating and to scare away whatever is threatening them. Just like when snakes hiss, other creatures probably know to stay away from this sound, as it's generally not associated with anything good (i.e., you're about to be bitten or pounced upon). By changing the shape of their tongue and pharynx (the tissue right in front of their voice box), cats are able to sharply release a jet of air while spitting some saliva in the process. As a veterinarian, I'm used to hearing that sound frequently (while I'm restraining cats or treating them), and I always proceed with caution. Be aware, cat lovers. If you've just approached a cat (or person) who's hissing at you, get the point and quickly back away.

How well do cats see in the dark, and why do they have vertical pupils?

Cats have evolved to become nocturnal hunters and are much more sensitive to light than humans, having "minimum light detection threshold up to [seven] times less than that of humans."[2] In addition, cats have vertical pupils to help finely control the amount of light coming into the back of their eye. Their pupil can become round or oval when dilated to allow more light in during the evening hours, making their night vision more accurate. Likewise, a vertical pupil can constrict down to a tiny, thin slit to prevent too much light from entering their eye during the day.

Ever wonder why your cat sometimes gets red-eye in photos? Well, cats have a *tapetum,* which is that reflective green, blue, or red hue in the back of their eye. This tapetum is 130 times more reflective than a human's.[3] Between having a higher sensitivity to light, a vertical pupil, a hyperactive tapetum, and a retina that has more rod photoreceptor cells (which help with visual acuity in low light) than cone cells (which help with color and detail), cats have exceptional night vision to help with their hunting prowess, or to attack your head at 3 A.M.

Do cats get cavities?

Because cats are strict carnivores, they typically don't crave anything but meat, meat, and meat (interspersed with the occasional catnip or cat grass); this meat is in the form of the star-, carrot-, ball-, nugget-, or fish-shaped dry kibble. Thankfully, cats don't typically want to eat chocolate, sweets, or acidic foods, so they are less likely to have saccharolytic acid-producing bacteria (in other words, the bacteria that causes cavities) in their mouths. Also, cats are lucky because their teeth don't have to last a century, since they unfortunately don't live as long as humans. (We humans have to make our teeth last until the denture discount kicks in!) Another reason cats rarely get cavities is because their teeth are just physically shaped differently from ours; cats have fewer nooks and crannies in their teeth in which to develop cavities. In fact, their sharp and razorlike teeth are designed to help rip and tear away at meat. This differs from the flat, occlusal surfaces on the teeth of omnivores (which are flat and designed to grind and chew). But, as you'll soon discover when you get Tigger's dental bill, cats develop feline oral resorptive lesions (FORLs) or cervical line lesions that require a lot of veterinary dental visits and teeth brushing at home. Just like how some people are more predisposed to a mouth full of cavities, the same with some cats; unfortunately, there's not much we can do to prevent them aside from routine oral care. While these FORLs aren't the same thing as cavities, they're similar—these lesions eat away at the gum, enamel, and dentin of the outside tooth, and make the pulp (the inside of the tooth where the nerves and blood vessels are) exposed and painful,[4] causing Tigger to get more finicky. If you notice redness of the gums, not eating, or severe halitosis, bring your cat to a vet to see if your cat needs dental work or extractions. Unfortunately for your wallet, you can only fix these by having your vet extract 'em, I'm afraid, no matter how much you brush or floss your cat's teeth.

Do cats have belly buttons?

You may have a hard time finding it under that huge fat pad, but your cat does have an *umbilicus*. Just like you and me, your cat had an umbilical cord that hooked him up to his mom's placenta for blood, nutrients, and waste exchange. The mother cat chews it off once her kittens are born. This chewing helps tie off the blood vessels, creating a belly button. Because there wasn't an obstetrician there to tie the knot, your kitten won't have an obvious innie or outie. If your cat's belly is shaved, you'll see a thin 1- to 2-centimeter scar, which is the belly button. If you see a fat little pouch (an outie), your cat may have an umbilical hernia that didn't heal right; most of the time, this needs to be surgically repaired and removed so intestines don't slip in the hernia and get stuck. Based on most cats that I've seen, their belly is so big, there's little room for anything but fat to slide in there!

Did curiosity kill the cat?

The question of why cats are so curious still remains a mystery to veterinarians. They didn't come up with that saying for nothing—curiosity did indeed kill the cat, but satisfaction brought her back. Because of their inquisitive and predatorial nature, cats often, but accidentally, put themselves in harm's way. It's not Chloe's fault that that little chipmunk ran up the tree and Chloe had to chase it, causing the fire department to come rescue her. Nobody told her that glue mousetrap was sticky. It's not her fault that the neighborhood bully didn't come with a warning sign. It's that playful nature that we love about our cats—just know that you may have to rescue them from their curiosity at times.

Does it hurt if my cat's whiskers get cut?

No, you won't hurt your cat's whiskers, or *vibrissae*, if they get accidentally cut. The whisker itself has no nerves or blood vessels but is firmly attached to a hair follicle and sinus, which has nerve innervation. (Ever accidentally yank out your nose hair? Ouch!) Your cat uses his whiskers as a sensing mechanism and air movement or vibrations allow him to "feel" where he is. You may notice your cat's whiskers are the width of your cat (or your cat's *ideal* width, I should say), which evolutionarily allows your cat to fit through tight spaces and sense how much personal space he has around him. Please don't cut those whiskers off—they are actually quite important to let him know how much room he has to wriggle!

Do cats fart?

Dogs (and men) fart. Cats (and women) don't. Yeah, right.

All right, ladies, admit it—we do actually *(ahem)* release odiferous essence after all. Cats are like women—we may fart, but it's quiet, polite, dignified, and never in public. While dogs (and men) may fart more loudly, rudely, and in public, cats are too majestic to do so. I've only ever heard Seamus fart once and was shocked—after all, cats are too prim and proper to grace us with their gas. Cats are generally fastidious creatures and always like to stay clean. They are constantly grooming, cleaning, and licking, but if you listen closely enough, it happens—and it may even stink. Cats are just smart enough to make you think Fido did it.

Why do cats shed?

Cats have hair for a reason—and it's not just to drive your allergic boyfriend nuts. That shedding hair *does* actually have a function. It helps protect your cat from the cold, heat, damaging UV rays, and biting arthropods (after all, those insects prefer your naked skin to getting a mouthful of fur!). It also acts as a protective barrier against any skin trauma that could occur while he's brawling with the neighborhood tomcat.

Since your little fuzzy fur ball doesn't have the option of donning a warm parka in the winter or getting buck-naked in the summer, your cat's coat has to be able to adapt to environmental changes. During short daylight, his brain maintains a thicker coat for warmth. In the spring and summer months, you may find yourself Swiffering your house much more frequently because during longer daylight hours, your cat's brain is affected by the changing photoperiod (the amount of daylight he is exposed to) and he may begin to shed more aggressively. For this reason, we vets don't advocate shaving cats that spend a lot of time outdoors, as they will (a) sunburn, (b) get attacked by insects, (c) get skin scrapes, and (d) get ridiculed by neighborhood tomcats.

There are three stages of hair growth: the growing period, the transitional period, and the resting period. Once the hair has gone through all these stages, it stays in the follicle as a dead hair until it is shed or removed by grooming or licking. Your cat then tries to help you out by purging all that dead hair on your Oriental carpet at 3 A.M. Remember that cats normally shed *some* of their coat to get rid of dead hair; however, if your cat starts going bald, or if you and your family start itching, bring your cat to a veterinarian and your family to the human dermatologist. While you should share your love with your cat, you don't want to share his fleas, mites, or ringworm. That said, don't blame your cat unnecessarily without good forensic evidence first. I once had a couple bring in their cat to be euthanized, as the couple was itching from their cat's "crabs"; upon further investigation, I concluded that apparently they had shed their *human crabs* to the cat, not vice versa! Gross! Thankfully, after a strict lesson on disease transmission, the cat was saved, and the owners were remorseful.

How do I make my cat shed less?

My non-vet friends always fearfully ask, "Is something wrong with your cat?" before they reach over to pet one of them. The thing is, I often shave Seamus and Echo (who are both short-haired) down to a peach-fuzz level. I do it because I can't stand the extra hair shedding in the house. Maybe it's not a typical, normal, healthy way to decrease shedding in the house during those spring and summer months, but hey, the veterinary clippers are just so accessible to this neat-freak mom! Don't worry—it's medically safe, especially since my cats are indoor only, so they aren't exposed to the elements, anyway. I should warn you, if you do attempt this, all your friends will make fun of you for having ugly-looking cats (but I still find them beautiful in their new lion-cut clip job).

There's not much else you can do to prevent your cats from shedding aside from constant brushing or grooming. While there are liquids, ointment, liniments, sprays, and other supplements advertised, don't believe the hype. The most important tip for minimizing shedding is to brush your cat daily (or at least weekly), particularly if he has medium to long hair. The more hair you brush or rake out (with those prickly, sharp, metal brushes), the less it will cling to your furniture, floor, fleece, and feet. There are a few breeds that don't shed, such as the Devon Rex or hairless Sphynx, but you have to get used to touching that greasy, ratlike skin that only a mother could love.

Why, when you shave your cat, does the hair grow back a different color?

Be aware that if you attempt to clip your cat's hair, it may grow back a different color or texture. Tigger's new shave job will still resemble his previous coat, but it may cause his undercoat to be thicker and his lines to be a bit less dramatic. Shaving Tigger may result in stimulation of an atypical coat pattern or change the normal three-staged life cycle of the hair follicle. I've slowly noticed that Seamus has less dramatic tabby lines after all my clip jobs. Don't get too excited—you can't make Tigger the tabby into a blond Himalayan.

Can I share clippers from my neighbor to shave my cat?

Because of the risk for sexually transmitted diseases, you don't share your "toys" with your friends and family, no matter how clean you think they may be, right? Likewise, I don't let anyone borrow my cat clippers. It sounds mean (hey, it's tough love), but there are a large percentage of cats that carry ringworm in their fur (which is the same fungus as athlete's foot) without ever showing symptoms. And I don't want my cats catching it from my friends' cats (or my friends' feet). Invest the few hundred dollars to get your own toy, uh, I mean clippers. It'd be so embarrassing to have to buy Tough Actin' Tinactin for your cat in front of all your friends.

Why do cats shed more at the vet?

Even the most courageous calico gets nervous at the veterinary clinic, and you may notice that she starts shedding massive amounts of hair—this is the flight-or-fight instinct kicking in. Not only does the heart rate increase from stress but the respiratory system also goes into overdrive—this is why she starts breathing harder in an attempt to get more oxygen into her lungs. Your cat's body is preparing for escape mode ("Help me! I smell dogs!"). At the same time, all the blood vessels and hair follicles are dilating to allow blood to flow to the escape muscles, and for this reason, hair may start to shed like mad. Don't worry too much (or your own hair may start to come out too); this should resolve itself shortly after you bring your cat home.

Why does my cat sleep so much?

Ah, the life of a cat. If we all took a few more catnaps during the week, we'd be a lot less stressed and cranky, don't you think?

Back before wildcats were domesticated into household pets, they were at the top of the food chain, so they didn't have to spend much time foraging for food, allowing them to sleep the rest of the day away. Typically, wildcats had short, fast bursts of hunting activity, and once done hunting, killing, and eating, they had the remainder of the day to lounge around. Since then, our domesticated cats have evolved so they can also lounge around for, say, sixteen hours a day. Since cats are nocturnal, you may not realize how much your cat sleeps during the day while you're hard at work. In fact, approximately 70 percent of your cat's life is spent napping. As an ER doctor working various shifts (from overnights to late nights to day shifts), I've always appreciated that Seamus and Echo slept with me during the day (after my overnight shift) without any disturbance. However, they get their revenge when I try to sleep at night (following a day shift)—playing, running, tackling each other, all around my head at 3 A.M. After sixteen hours of resting all day, they get bored in the wee hours of the morning. Can you blame them?

Are all cats good mousers?

I'd be lying if I told you all cats were good for something. Don't adopt a cat because you have a mouse problem; rather, adopt a cat because you want to enjoy his or her company for the next ten to twenty years. Not all cats are good mice catchers, so you may be stuck with a poor mouser. Unfortunately, there's no behavioral, prescreening, test-drive ability (or return policy) to find out if the cat you're about to adopt is a good mouser or not. It's all in the genes, I'm afraid. Not all of us are the quarterback jock with good hand-eye coordination. My cat Echo is a great hunter. I keep him indoors so he doesn't kill anything, but all the crawling bugs and moths that make it in the house meet a quick demise. My other cat, Seamus, is fatter and lazier and has stared at mice and neither moved nor cared. Could be you might just adopt a really fat, lazy cat.

Why do cats like to be at the highest place in the room but then act like they're afraid of heights?

Ever notice how your cat likes to hang out behind you, lying on top of the tallest sofa or chair in the room? Our domesticated cats like to climb and often prefer to be at the highest point—you know, on top of the refrigerator, on the kitchen counter, or sitting on top of your computer monitor, distracting you as you work. This lets them enjoy a bird's-eye view of the room to make sure they can keep track of everyone and everything going on and gives them a different perspective on things. If you're one of those cool owners who has a cat-walk near the ceiling of your house, your cat doesn't know how lucky he or she is!

When cats lounge around up there, they are like that lazy panther or jaguar, just chilling out in the forest, waiting for something to pounce on, while resting in those high tree branches. This lets them safely rest and watch the world go by. Housecats that get to explore outdoors are more likely to get themselves into a pickle—only to find out that maybe they are afraid of heights, after all. Turns out our domesticated cats like to climb trees but haven't quite figured out how to get back down as elegantly as a panther. Clueless Chloe doesn't mind going higher and higher until she realizes that she's too much of a 'fraidy cat to come back down from the top of a forty-foot tree. So, there may be some cats who realize that they enjoy being on top of the world, but since "curiosity killed the cat," they soon learn that the firefighter has to bring them back . . .

Do cats always land on their feet?

Warning: do not throw your cat up in the air to see if he lands on his feet! Cats are very agile creatures, and they will jump from a counter or tree branch to catch a toy or a bird. While many cats appear to graciously land on their feet, there are some cats that get severely injured from what we veterinarians term "high-rise syndrome."

Feline high-rise syndrome describes those curious cats that lean and fall out of your apartment window from at least two stories high. Tigger may have just wandered near the window to check out the bugs through the screen, and before you know it, curiosity abounds him and he accidentally falls through. Not surprising, the majority of cats that succumb to high-rise syndrome are young (averaging two to three years of age), dumb, and male (76 percent).[5] I guess young, male cats are a bit more reckless and clueless (just like their two-legged counterparts). What veterinarians have found is that the average fall is typically four stories, and thankfully, the majority of cats (more than 95 percent) survive. Unfortunately, more than a third sustain leg fractures or chest trauma (such as fractured ribs, lung bruises, or air leakage from their lungs).[6] Understandably, the higher the fall (i.e., more than six or seven stories), the more severe the injuries. (Doesn't take a veterinarian to have to tell you that, huh?) Being that your average fracture repair and ER visit will cost you between $2,000 and $3,500, help prevent this potentially fatal error by making sure your high-rise windows are all tightly fastened and kid- or cat-proof.

That said, cats appear to naturally land on their feet for several reasons. First, cats reach terminal velocity (which is when the downward force of gravity equals the upward force of drag, resulting in a constant speed) at a much faster rate than your average human skydiver. In fact, veterinarians estimate that cats reach terminal velocity at approximately five stories. Cats also have a strong "righting" reflex, which means they can twist and turn themselves into the "right" position until they are correct side up. Because cats are flexible and agile, they have the ability to fan themselves out (by extending their arms and legs) to increase their surface area to minimize the fall. But as you noticed from the studies above, not all cats land on their feet. Avoid the problem and help preserve the other eight lives of your cat: close your window!

Why do cats prefer to drink running water?

Cats are curious creatures by nature and enjoy playing in water while staying *mostly* dry. My mother, who isn't a cat person, once called me in dismay while pet-sitting Seamus; she explained that she had to leave the bathroom sink on a slow drip to get him to drink enough water. Otherwise, she never saw Seamus at the water bowl and was worried he was getting dehydrated. I reminded her that cats are desert creatures; they have specially designed kidneys (extra-long loops of Henle, if you really must know) to help concentrate their urine and absorb as much water from their kidneys as they can. For that reason, you hardly ever see cats sitting at the water bowl as much as a dog does. Personally, I know that Seamus loves to run into the bathroom after I'm done showering to lick up all the extra water. While his kidneys are fine, he likes the variety of different-tasting water (maybe he likes the essence of Dove body cleaner) from a different surface. No need to freak out and leave every faucet on for your cat—that would dramatically increase your water bill and make Al Gore very upset. Most times, healthy cats prefer to drink out of a dripping faucet just for variety, although a plain bowl of clean, fresh water will suffice just fine.

If, however, you notice that (a) your older cat is hovering constantly by the water bowl, (b) he is trying to lift the toilet seat to get a drink, (c) the clumps in the litter box are bigger than the size of your head (or his!), or (d) you're constantly refilling his dish, bring him to a veterinarian for some blood work and urine testing to nip any medical problems in the bud. That's because there are some diseases such as diabetes, hyperthyroidism, kidney failure, or feline lower urinary tract disease where thirst and water balance (and hence your cat's ability to stay hydrated) are impacted; in these situations, it's imperative to treat the underlying disease and also to ensure that your cat is drinking even more water than normal. Since some cats will drink *more* out of kitty water fountains (where the water is constantly trickling, like a melodic stream), these gadgets are beneficial if your cat happens to have any of those scary-sounding diseases above. I'd recommend that you run out to your local pet store to get a fountain if your cat is diagnosed with one of these medical conditions—it's worth it!

Do cats like to swim?

Don't you dare let your boyfriend read this and think he can put your cat into the tub or swimming pool—that is, unless your kitty is a Turkish Van. This unique breed of cat has been recognized by the Cat Fanciers' Association since the mid-1990s and is one of the only cats that actually *chooses* to play in the water. Because these cats were bred near Lake Van in eastern Turkey, they have passed on their swimming gene that makes them the Michael Phelps of cats. Not to be confused with the Turkish Angora, the Van has ultrasoft, quick-drying fur that helps them regain their hairdo and composure immediately after a dip.

All other non-Van cats usually despise swimming and generally prefer not to be tortured with a bath. While cats may be curious and want to dip their paw in water, most prefer to stay dry and don't actually want to be completely immersed. I mean, the indignity! How dare you mess up their hair! Most cats descended from the desert regions of the world, where they didn't routinely go for a swim. While some wild, large cats (such as tigers) love to swim and frolic in the water to cool off, most other large cats like panthers and lions don't want to stick their head underwater; they'll only swim to get from point A to point B, or to catch their next meal.

Why are orange tabbies almost always male while calicos and tortoiseshells are always female?

The majority of the time, orange and white tabby (striped) cats are male, while calico (orange or black, with white large "piebalding" patches) or tortoiseshell cats (varieties of white, black, and orange with no white patches) are female. This is due to the complicated sex-linked color gene.

Before we get into sex and genes and colors, know that

some veterinarians are cat color biased. For years, veterinarians had mysteriously hypothesized that these color patterns were also linked to the friendliness gene. Interestingly enough, we may now have the scientific research to support this veterinary old wives' tale: one recent study has shown that when domesticated foxes were bred for friendliness, their coat color got mangier and uglier. Based on this study,[7] many believe that coat color is associated with hormones that may make an animal nicer.

I personally believe that orange tabbies are the most outgoing and lovable of all the cat colors while the calico cats are the "queen" of the bunch. ("Please don't touch me. You're *disturbing* me.") If you really must know, calico cats often seem to be the meanest, most feisty cats while in the hospital. Don't get me wrong—they may be wonderful angels at home, but they put up the worst fight at the veterinarian. Your veterinarian probably doesn't tell you that once your female feline is at the vet clinic, she pretty much becomes, well, a vicious, drooling, ferocious tiger who's trying to rip everyone's eyes out (no, seriously). Whether or not it's because she's a female, or owing to the genetic link between friendliness and coat color, she'll turn into a biting, scratching, screaming, vicious land shark when your veterinarian takes her into the back room. Most vet techs and vets have a healthy respect for these frenzied females. We're talking drugs (chemical restraint), nets, leather gloves, muzzles, towels, fur flying, chasing, and so on. In fact, if you have a cat this color and know that she's bad when you bring her to the vet, do us all a favor. Arrange to pick up oral sedatives first—it will make everyone's life easier!

Color favoritism aside, veterinarians know that most orange and white tabbies are male, while most calicos and "torties" are female. Coat coloration is very complex as it is influenced by many genes and their genetic status as dominant or recessive (which is the strength in ability to be expressed). There are several alleles for each color, described as O for the orange allele (which is the dominant color gene, resulting in the orange color), or o for the black allele (which is the recessive color gene, resulting in non-orange fur). These colors are considered sex linked, as they are associated with the female X chromosome: the O gene is located on the X chromosome, and if you recall your tenth-grade science lessons about Mendel's peas, you'll recall the males are XY while females are XX. In other words, since males only carry one X chromosome, they are more likely to have orange fur since it's also a dominant gene. Since o is recessive, it requires an oo combination to result in a non-orange color, while Oo yields the tortoiseshell color. To achieve the calico color, O and o both need to be expressed on the female X chromosome, and being that males only have one X chromosome, the majority of calicos are female (more than 90 percent). Voilà! So, go ahead and skip eight years of veterinary schooling and sex your new kitten based on its coloring. If you just adopted a kitten, hedge your bets and pick out your favorite boy names for orange tabbies and girl names for calico or tortie cats. If you ever see a male calico or tortoiseshell, you are (a) lucky or (b) the proud owner of a possible XXY animal, which you can name Hermie. (Congratulations—owning a hermaphrodite is quite rare!) While color coat expression is very complicated, know that orange tabbies are almost always male, while calicos and torties are almost always female.

Are black cats bad luck?

Being an owner of an all-black cat, I personally don't believe the hype and superstition around their color. Part of this superstition may have started as early as the reign of King Charles I of England, who adored his black cat so much that he had it under protection and tight guard. When it died, King Charles was coincidentally arrested the following day, and the superstition of bad luck may have started after that. Compounded by that, old folklore stated that fishermen's wives used to keep black cats at home to keep their men safe at sea, so black cats were often stolen owing to their coveted value. Sailors believed that if a black cat approached you on the boat, it was good luck, but if a black cat approached you and turned away, you were doomed to bad luck. Legend also had it that witches could transform into black cats, causing people to fear them. That said, should we fear black cats in modern day?

As a veterinarian, I personally feel that orange and white tabby males rank first for friendliness, followed by black males coming in as a close second. Calicos come in last for friendliness (see "Why are orange tabbies almost always male while calicos and tortoiseshells are always female?" in this chapter), at least at the veterinary clinic, with gray long-haired cats being the most shy. Of course, I don't have the scientific data to prove it (there is none!), but in my biased opinion, black is beautiful.

Why does my cat like NASCAR?

You may notice that your cat likes to chase any fast-moving object running around on a TV screen with zest. Some cats seem to pay attention more, while others could care less. With their strong instinctive, predatorial drive, some cats may view TV as a free opportunity to sharpen their skills. If your cat responds to the chirping birds or the darting NASCAR the way my dog does to the doorbell ringing on TV, then sure, leave your TV on for your cat when you go to work if it makes you feel better (just check with your husband to make sure he doesn't mind kitty-litter-dusted paw prints on the new plasma screen). While your cat doesn't have a personal preference for Tony Stewart or Bobby Labonte, your cat does for rapidly moving objects. I believe that the waste of electricity may not be worth it, and a good ten-minute exercise time when you get home instead may be more mentally and physically stimulating for your kitty. That way you can save the earth and your cat's waist size at the same time!

Why do cats like laser pointers? Will they go blind from them?

Don't worry—no one will accuse you of trying to take down a plane while you're playing with your cat's laser pointer (mature adults only, please). Laser pointers are great, cheap cat toys, and they can drive your cat insane with happiness or frustration. Playing with a laser pointer helps increase the amount of exercise your fat, indoor cat may be getting (see "How do I exercise my fat, indoor cat?" in chapter 5). One particularly dedicated cat owner actually patented the idea of using a laser pointer as a form of cat exercise (United States Patent 5,443,036).[8] Apparently I wasn't the only one who thought this was taking it a bit too far (patent envy, anyone?). Society's Big Brother of patents, freepatentsonline.com, was watching and listed this patent on their list of crazy, silly patent ideas out there.[9]

Depending on the strength of the laser pointer (which is usually greater than 5 mW), retina damage could potentially occur if the laser is pointed directly into the eye. Thankfully, constant blinking may decrease the incidence of eye injury, but your cat may not realize this while playing ("Blink, Felix, blink!"). In general, only shine your laser pointer at the ground (no high-flying airplanes) and avoid your cat's eyes.

Are Siamese cats ever identical?

Siamese cats date back to the late 1800s and originated from Siam (present-day Thailand, for all you non–geography buffs). This unique, beautiful cat breed is known for its cream to dark brown coloring and almond-shaped blue eyes and was made famous by their notable "Siamese Cat Song": "We are Siamese, if you please!" in the Disney movie *Lady and the Tramp*. If you are about to be the proud owner of a Siamese, you should be prepared to hear this cry (constantly), as this breed is very talkative and chatty.

The term "Siamese twins" generally refers to human twins that failed to separate, and the origin of this term was likely made famous in the early 1800s. Chang Bunker and Eng Bunker (May 11, 1811–January 17, 1874), who descended from Chinese Cham parents, were born in Siam and were conjoined twins stuck together by some skin, cartilage, and a shared liver.[10] After traveling with the Barnum circus and being labeled as "Siamese twins," the term stuck. While the country of origin was similar for the first Siamese human conjoined twins and breed of cat, no, Siamese cats are not identical.

What in the world is anal atresia?

Cool words to use at the next cocktail party: apoptosis (programmed cell death), neural crest cell, and anal atresia. Could be that medical people are just really geeky, but hey . . .

Anal atresia is, sadly, the congenital (inherited) lack of an anus or an appropriately sized anus. Sometimes a small dimple may be evident instead of an opening. This becomes pretty obvious (surprisingly, most people don't naturally look for a butt hole) a few days after your kitty's birth. You may start to notice that the mom cat isn't grooming the new kitten, that he isn't defecating, and that he's developing a bigger and bigger pot-bellied abdomen (since poop isn't being defecated out . . . talk about a bad case of constipation). Surgical intervention is mandatory as soon as possible. This is sometimes seen in day-old kittens or calves, although it can affect all species. Bum-mer—literally.

Why do Manx cats lack a tail?

While some dog breeds have their tails docked (or surgically removed according to breed standards), some cats naturally lack a tail. Of course, some cats lose their tails owing to near escapes or because of those darn rocking chairs (ouch!). If you are a Manx cat, however, you can blame the neural crest cell for your anatomically absent appendage. Apparently, these early developmental nerve cells are quite important, as they result in the normal development of the spinal cord, backbone, and tail. Without these neural crest cells, you get no tail, resulting in a Manx cat. While you may think Groucho's stub of a tail is cute, these abnormal cell defects can sometimes result in severe, life-threatening deformities like spina bifida (an incompletely formed spinal cord or spinal canal), anal atresia (no butt hole), or fecal incontinence (no fun for anyone!); unfortunately, none of these problems has an easy cure. That said, if you see a tailless Manx cat in the shelter, you may think he's a cute one to adopt; just make sure he wasn't surrendered for fecal incontinence. Hopefully, he had a prior surgery to amputate his tail (like if he was hit by a car or got his tail stuck in a door) and has a working anal sphincter (which usually means he isn't fecally incontinent). Don't worry—your veterinarian will check to make sure this part of your new cat works well.

Is it true cats have two pairs of eyelids?

Cats have a total of three eyelids: the top and bottom lids that help Felix blink and an extra third eyelid, tucked inside the corner of the eye. This third eyelid is called a *nictitans* and is basically an extra layer of protection for the cornea. Cats like to fight with neighboring cats; this extra eyelid acts as a shield to protect the cornea. Sometimes the third eyelid can become elevated with trauma (such as a corneal ulcer, which is a scratch on the clear surface of the eye) or can pop up with general malaise (from severe dehydration or weight loss) or infections (such as upper respiratory viruses). You normally shouldn't see the third eyelid at all, but if it pops up, something is wrong, and you should take your cat to a vet for closer inspection.

Does my cat listen when I talk?

While you may not think so, your cat actually *does* listen to your voice, at least the *pitch* of your voice. What we don't know is whether or not your cat comprehends what you're saying or if he *cares* to comprehend. Both Seamus and Echo recognize their names and will come when called, but anything more than that is like talking to my boyfriend during a football game. Unlike dogs, cats don't have the same drive to seek human approval, so they don't need to pretend to listen to you. Dogs were originally bred for specific purposes (such as catching your dinner, protecting your sheep, or guarding you and your loved ones) and, as a result, are very voice or command oriented. In other words, those that didn't listen to owners or who weren't responsive to obeying commands probably didn't have their genes propagated in the breeding pool (after all, if your dog couldn't catch a rabbit and just ran away from you, you probably weren't going to continue to breed him as a hunting dog). Cats were bred to catch mice and look good back in the old Egyptian days and have succeeded in both since then—without having to listen to you in the process.

Why do cats like to lie exactly where you are reading?

Cats love to be the center of attention without actually being the center of attention—in other words, they want to be right where you can see them but not where you can *touch* them. If you think about it, you often have a pile of newspapers lying in the corner on the floor. Do you ever see your cat lying on them? Nope—not unless you are trying to read them at the kitchen table. So it's not that your cat wants to actually lie on a different surface for fun—your cat just wants you to realize that he's right there for you, supporting your every read.

Why do cats arch their backs?

Cats arch their backs for several reasons. When Seamus is getting up from catnapping in a sunbeam, it's his way of stretching his epaxial and lower back muscles. When I gently give Seamus "butt smacks," as I lovingly call them, he arches his rear up in pleasure—he wants more scratches on his lower back, at the base of his tail. That's the equivalent of our getting a free back massage. If, however, you notice your cat arching his back, hissing, fluffing his fur, and trying to look bigger and scarier, he's scared and may be trying to intimidate that neighborhood cat, dog, or chipmunk until it backs off.

Why do cats like to sleep in the sun?

The normal body temperature of a cat is between 100°F and 102.5°F, and your cat is able to maintain that regardless of how cheap you are with your heat or your air conditioner. Your cat isn't lying in the sunlight to warm up—it's just the equivalent of you wanting to go outside and lie out on a nice, sunny day. That sunbeam just feels so good. Feels great to have that fur warmed up—it's like a hot stone therapy spa for a cat.

In the rare circumstance that your cat is constantly heat seeking, however, beware. Although it's extremely rare, it could be that his thyroid is underactive (this is sometimes a problem after treatment for hyperthyroidism, an *over*active thyroid gland), and now he has a slower metabolic rate. Either that, or he really just prefers the sunbeam (and you turning up the heat in your house).

Why does cat pee stink worse than dog pee?

For those of you who have ever fostered a tomcat or had an alley cat in your backyard, you can attest to the fact that cat pee reeks way more than dog pee! But why? Cats have much stronger concentrated urine than dogs. The normal concentration of urine is based on *specific gravity* (often abbreviated "sp. gr." or "spgr," for those really lazy vets, such as myself), which measures the density of a liquid (i.e., how concentrated that liquid is). Using a simple tool called a refractometer, your veterinarian can check the concentration of your cat's urine. Normal cat urine specific gravity is greater than 1.040, while a dog's specific gravity is normally 1.020 to 1.040. This may sound like a lot of medical mumbo jumbo, but what it boils down to is that dogs have much more dilute urine, which means that it is less foul, less concentrated, and less yellow in color than cats'.

Cats have such concentrated urine because they originated from the desert and have very long loops of Henle, the part of the kidney that results in filtration and concentration.

While you too have a loop of Henle (*très romantique!*), yours isn't as long as your cat's, so you don't usually concentrate your urine quite as much (unless you're hiking in the woods and not hydrating adequately!). As a result, cats absorb a large amount of water from their urine to maintain their hydration, which also explains why you hardly ever see them drink—they're so effective at concentrating! A cat's loop of Henle is so good at squeezing every last drop of absorbable water out that this concentration makes the urine smell quite foul. The good news is that it comes with some benefits: not only do cats urinate less than dogs (can you imagine scooping a litter box for a dog?), but it's also a lot harder for bacteria to grow in their bladder with such a concentrated fluid. Sometimes this can result in problems if your cat has a history of developing bladder crystals. The more concentrated the urine is, the more concentrated the crystals become, which could turn into a bladder stone. For more information on feline lower urinary tract disease, see "How often do I *really* need to clean my cat's litter box?" in chapter 3.

Male cats that have not been fixed have the added effect of testosterone, which makes their urine ten times more stinky. You can minimize the occurrence of this foul urine in your cat's litter box or the behavioral problems of marking (spraying disgusting urine all over the walls of your house) by neutering your cat before eight to nine months of age.

If you notice your cat's urine is too dilute, not typically as foul as usual, or if the urine clumps in the litter box are getting too large, contact a veterinarian, as this is often a sign of underlying kidney disease, thyroid problems, or even diabetes (see "How big of a clump is normal?" in chapter 3). Your cat isn't trying to drink more than eight glasses of water a day just to alleviate your sense of smell when you pull litter box duty, so something may be wrong.

Why do cats follow you into the bathroom?

Well, it's not for your odiferous habits. Despite their strong sense of smell, cats seem to tolerate your stink and love to follow you into the bathroom. Some people hypothesize that it's because cats don't like being shut out of a section of the house, and as soon as that door closes they want in to investigate what's going on behind closed doors. I think that cats know that they have you trapped, like a mouse stuck on a glue trap. They know you can't go anywhere while you're sitting on the john, and now you *have* to pet them. Now they can rub their face all over your legs and you can't move or resist because you're stuck. At least you know they love you and your smells.

Chapter 2
CURIOSITY KILLED THE CAT

JUST graduated from college, secured your first job, bought your first town house, and furnished it with a bunch of IKEA furniture? Ready for the next household item—in other words, *thinking about getting a cat*? Maybe you're thinking about adopting a new kitten or purchasing an expensive purebred cat but never owned your own cat before as a full-fledged, quasi-responsible adult. Maybe you innately love cats but aren't sure if you're ready to commit to having one for the next fifteen to twenty years (don't you dare return Tigger to the shelter after ten years!). If you're a novice cat owner, you should definitely read this chapter before getting that cat—see what you need to learn before you commit. Read on, because this is the insider's guide to cat ownership!

Maybe you're one of my favorite clients: those who own a

few of each pet (you can probably guess why, based on Seamus, JP, and Echo). Then you probably (erroneously) think that one "dog" year still equals seven years, even for cats, right? You may think you know how to medicate a cat, since you know how to stick a pill in a piece of hot dog for Fido. Think you can use those bulky, cold metal guillotine dog nail clippers on your cat's nails? Boy, are you wrong.

Pet curious? Maybe you don't have any pets and aren't quite sure if you're a cat or dog person. Some people innately know based on what pets they grew up with. Like I mentioned before, I spend more time with dogs because I'm an outdoorsy type, but I still own and adore cats. Seamus was my "experimental adoption," and as my first official cat, he helped teach me everything about cats that I didn't learn in veterinary school—I've been lovin' him ever since.

For you experienced cat owners, notice how as soon as you whip out that Sherpa carrier, your cat takes off, hides in a closet, and holds on for dear life while tearing your nice silk dress and pissing on your Manolo Blahnik strappy sandals in the process? Cats are smarter than you think, and they remember that last vet visit like it happened yesterday. Rest assured, your friendly feline veterinarian isn't trying to torture your cat (I promise!), but sometimes cats just don't understand. The following are answers your veterinarian wants you to know but may not have time to explain in that fifteen-minute appointment. In this chapter, find out why your cat is running away from veterinary answers that you seek.

Am I a cat person or a dog person?

In general, cats are more independent and require less commitment. They like to be around you but expect you to feed and pet them only when they want. Cats offer great companionship, along with the relaxing, blood-pressure-lowering sounds of purring and the added bonus of bulimic hair ball releasing onto your carpet at 3 A.M. They do well in apartments and small living quarters, but do need routine veterinary care (such as annual exams), even if they aren't exposed to the great outdoors or other cats. With cats, you can leave for a short weekend without the involved commitment of hiring a pet-sitter to come by two or three times a day. Cats, on average, live for fifteen to twenty years, so if you cannot commit to a pet for that long, do not get one!

Dogs, on the other hand, are much more of a high commitment companion. Not only do dogs need to be walked three times a day, but they need someone to responsibly pick up after them, feed and water them, play with them, and sleep with them. When in doubt about how much commitment you have to offer, be aware that dogs are a lot of work. Of course, their companionship, friendship, and loyalty are well worth it, but if you can't provide the time and energy to be with them, it's not time for you to have a dog yet. Plus, as any cat would tell you, dogs drool and cats rule.

Is one cat year really equivalent to seven human years?

While people think that one dog year equals seven human years, that's not exactly true, and it doesn't hold for cats either. There's no rule on this 1:7 age ratio, nor is there accurate scientific data on this topic. Remember that different species or breeds age at different rates, as weight, obesity, nutrition, genetics, and environmental factors may play a role. While this formula acts as a good general guideline, it is more likely to be inaccurate in the age extremes: very young or very old pets. For example, a one-year-old cat may have reached "puberty," but this doesn't correlate to a seven-year-

DOGS				CATS	
AGE (YEARS)	SMALL BREED	MEDIUM BREED	LARGE BREED	AGE (YEARS)	HUMAN EQUIVALENT
1	15	15	15	6 mths	10
2	24	24	24	1	15
3	28	28	28	2	24
4	32	32	32	3	28
5	36	36	36	4	32
6	40	42	45	5	36
7	44	47	50	6	40
8	48	51	55	7	44
9	52	56	61	8	48
10	56	60	66	9	52
11	60	65	72	10	56
12	64	69	77	11	60
13	68	74	82	12	64
14	72	78	88	13	68
15	76	83	93	14	72
16	80	87	120	15	76
17	84	92		16	82
18	88	96		17	84
19	92	101		18	88
20				19	92
21				20	96
				21	100

IDEXX Comparative Age Chart[1] (see Resources)

old girl. Likewise, many cats can commonly live until fifteen to twenty years of age. This correlates to a 105- to 140-year-old human, and there aren't many humans who live to age 140. In general, one cat year is most equivalent to seven human years in the "middle-aged" years only.

The first year of life is equivalent to a youth (approximately a fifteen-year-old), while a two-year-old cat is equivalent to a young adult (approximately a twenty-four-year-old). After that, each year is equivalent to approximately five human years. I like to group ages into broader categories: infant, toddler, child, adolescent, young adult, adult, middle-aged, elderly, geriatric, and uh, dead. Because this is factor dependent, the most important thing to remember is that as your cat ages, so will its body, so make sure to keep up with those geriatric checkups at your veterinarian. Otherwise, check out the age comparison chart on the previous page and the Antech and IDEXX websites.

How many cats are too many?

Do we really need to answer this question?

Unfortunately, we do. You may hear of the occasional crazy "hoarder" revealed on the news—people who live with a hundred cats hidden in their house (and hopefully nowhere near your neighborhood).[2] Sadly for the cats, the m.o. of your cat-lovin', urine-smelling, disheveled animal hoarder is quite sad. Most hoarders are unmarried and live alone (and you thought it was hard to find a date with just two cats!). Hoarders also come from all different socioeconomic backgrounds and are typically over sixty years of age. To top it off, over three-quarters of hoarders are female, once again giving the single, white female a bad rep. In 69 percent of hoarding cases, animal urine and feces were found accumulated in living areas. If you think that's bad, know that more than one in four hoarders' beds are also soiled with animal crap—makes you not want to date and lie with one, I suppose. Sadly, 80 percent of reported cases had dead or sick animals present in the house, and 60 percent of the time hoarders didn't acknowledge the problem. Finally, cats seem to be the overall species "loser" in these cases—over 65 percent of cases of animal hoarding involved cats, although some also hoard small dogs and rabbits.[3]

While this book is unlikely to be in a hoarder's library, we as veterinarians usually recommend no more than four to five cats. Sometimes I offend my fellow veterinarians, technicians, and friends when I tell them my cutoff for crazy is six cats. After that, you're somewhat of a lunatic. Of course, if you ask ten different vets, you may get ten different answers. That said, until those nine other vets write an opinionated book about it, I still recommend no more than four or five cats per household. Animal behavior specialists often see more problems in multicat households. Having too many cats may result in urination problems (i.e., not in the litter box!), intercat fighting and attacking, and difficulty in monitoring general health. For example, checking the litter box to see if one cat has a urinary tract infection is more difficult when you have six cats. Second, though I love my house *and* my pets, I prefer not to have pee in the corners of my carpeted basement—but hey, that's just me.

So how many cats should you get? I have to say that I enjoyed having a one-cat household—Seamus was more friendly and affectionate to humans (more to the point, me!) as an only child. Since adopting Echo, I've seen less of Seamus. Now they just want to play together (constantly). I've been officially demoted to the source of food and to litter box duty. Now my two cats play, wrestle, and chase each other and generally prefer to do this around my head at 3 A.M. while I'm trying to sleep. The good news is that Seamus's quality of life, social skills, and exercise level have improved. Unfortunately, I sleep less as a result. Luckily, I get my feline revenge by waking them up randomly at 2 P.M. ("Wakey, wakey!") while they are resting in a sunbeam taking a catnap ("I'm sorry, were you sleeping?"). That said, two cats, one dog, and lots of backyard rabbits and birds are plenty for me in my 700-square-foot house . . .

Is it better to get a kitten or an adult?

I'm guilty of both: I adopted Seamus as a kitten and Echo as an adult. In actuality, I'm a huge advocate of adopting adult cats, as shelters have a harder time finding homes for them. Most people want cute, cuddly, playful little kittens as they are typically more fun to have around; therefore, kittens typically get scooped up and quickly adopted at the shelter, leaving those poor "less than desirable" young adults out there. Keep in mind when you get that kitten that they are extremely mischievous and very active, so if you're seeking a couch potato companion, you're better off adopting an adult cat. Young kittens also require a bit of training, as you may need to show them how to use a scratching post or how to use the litter box. That said, cats are only kittens once, and if you have the tenacity, time, and energy to do so, adopting a kitten would be a fun way of bonding with your new four-legged friend. But if you're not set on a kitten and willing to adopt an older cat, go for it—your veterinarian and humane society will be *really* proud of you. You likely just saved and extended Frisky's life.

Should I get a short-haired cat or a long-haired cat?

Can't decide between a short- or long-haired cat? Your preference for hair length should be dependent on how often you like to brush cats, clean up hair balls, groom, or vacuum. The type of cat you adopt affects how often you will have to brush and care for all that hair. I'll admit it, long-haired cats are beautiful, soft, and silky. But, these cats need to be brushed at least weekly to make sure they don't develop hair balls or mats (which are painful and difficult to remove once they've formed, quashing my desire to ever get dreadlocks). Unfortunately, long-haired cats don't fit in my busy lifestyle. I honestly can barely care for my own hair, and I don't have time to groom a long-haired cat once a week. Seamus and Echo are both short haired (and even shorter when I groom them), and I love them for it.

If you're thinking about getting a long-haired cat, realize that there's a lot of work involved with all that hair. Finally, ask yourself if you're OK with the occasional hair ball purge all over your house. If you're not, adopt a short-haired cat or groom your cat into the lion cut frequently. While most hair balls pass into the feces without complication, they can occasionally result in vomiting or an expensive obstruction resulting in surgery. You could buy a whole lot of lion cuts for that price.

Are purebred cats better?

Just like purebred dogs, there are some beautiful, wonderful purebred cats out there. Depending on what traits, coat patterns, color, size, or characteristics you are specifically looking for, there are many types of cats to choose from. Unlike dogs, cats aren't used for specific purposes, which is a good thing, because I don't know if I'd want to adopt a working breed (police cat, anyone?) versus a non-herding cat. Regardless, some people may have breed preferences for certain personality types. That said, be an aware and well-educated consumer when looking for a purebred; as with purebred dogs, there are certain diseases, such as feline infectious peritonitis, feline leukemia, or genetically inherited defects (such as heart defects or polycystic kidneys), from possible inbreeding that may be more common in less savory, purebred catteries where appropriate screening and testing may not be done. Before purchasing a purebred, research the breed thoroughly and seek veterinary advice to make sure you are making an educated and well-thought-out decision. If you don't have a preference, know that you can find whatever color, breed, size, sex, or pattern standard domestic short- or long-haired cat from the shelter, so look around and explore your options.

What breed is best for me? What are the most popular varieties of purebred cats?

While there are limited "what breed of cat am I" quizzes on the Internet, they just aren't the same as the dog quizzes. They don't actually quiz you to see what breed you would turn out to be if you were reincarnated as a cat (I'm a Siamese because I'm Asian?); rather, they quiz you to see if you know the origin and history of the cat (I'm proud to say that I scored an 80 percent but only after doing research for this book).

Still not sure? Not to encourage you to follow the crowd, but the top ten most popular cats, as reported by Cat Fanciers' Association (CFA) in 2006, are listed below. Being a pessimistic veterinarian (Sorry, but I'm only looking out for you and your cat), I've also included the most common genetic problems inherent in the breed—not saying all of the cats get these, but just so you know what to look out for!

1. **Persian:** Persians are known for their smooshed face, runny eyes, chronic sneezing, occasional snoring, and high-maintenance long hair (which means you have to brush Princess frequently). Despite all that, they're popular for a reason—it's a face only a mother could love. The bad news is that this breed does have an inherited kidney problem called polycystic kidney disease, which means their kidneys become filled with nonfunctioning cysts, which results in severe life-threatening kidney failure at an early age.

2. **Maine Coon:** Maine Coon cats are one of my favorites—stocky and big boned with beautiful long hair, they are also very affectionate. They are the gentle giants of the cat species but also require extensive grooming and brushing. Unfortunately, hypertrophic cardiomyopathy is inherited in this breed and found most commonly in young male Maine Coons. This is the same type of heart disease that causes NBA basketball players to occasionally fall over dead, and causes their heart muscle to become too thick and inefficient.

3. **Exotic:** The Exotic is also known as the lazy man's Persian. Exotics look just like Persians and have similar personalities with less work involved. Perfect! Their short hair requires less grooming than the Persian's and they still have that face only their mother (or father!) could love.

4. **Siamese:** Siamese cats were very popular in the 1980s, thanks to the release of *Lady and the Tramp*. The two Siamese were classically displayed in this Disney movie—chatty, elegant, and very vocal. Lonely in that big house of yours? The cries of a Siamese will quickly fill it (all the time), as they follow you from room to room seeking your affection. Asthma and diabetes mellitus are seen more commonly in this breed, so word to the wise—if you smoke or tend to let your cats get obese (and hate needles or giving injections twice a day), this may not be the breed for you.

5. **Abyssinian:** I personally think Abyssinians are the most beautiful—they have that unique ruddy brown coat (although they come in multiple colors) and are extremely affectionate. This breed looks like the original, royal, elegant, Egyptian cat that was worshipped. They are active acrobats and are often found jumping around on top of your refrigerator and furniture. A rare life-threatening disease called amy-

loidosis, which results in abnormal tissue infiltrating their organs, is found in this breed, although it's been less prevalent recently. This is the breed that I'm on the Abyssinian Rescue waiting list for!

6. **Ragdoll:** The Ragdoll sounds like its name—when you pick them up, they lie there, limp like a ragdoll. They are the Bob Marley of the cat breed—laid back, tranquil, and mellow.

7. **Birman:** The Birman looks like a long-haired Siamese-Persian with white front paws. Originally from Burma, the Khmer people considered this cat sacred, as they lived in the temples with Kittah priests. Like any breed of cat, they want to be treated like royalty!

8. **American Shorthair:** The American Shorthair may be the only cat that fits in the "working breed," if such categories for cat breeds existed. These cats descended from those on the original *Mayflower* and were used to keep the rodent population down on the boats. While there is a lot of variation in this breed, they are most famous for that dramatic black tabby appearance.

9. **Oriental:** The Oriental cat lends itself to over 300 types of variety, but originates from the Siamese cat and is very similar in personality (but maybe slightly less vocal). You can pretty much pick any color or make that you want.

10. **Sphynx:** Don't like cat fur? Get a bald Sphynx instead. This breed was started in 1966 when a domestic shorthair produced a bald kitten, and since then the breed has propagated. Very unique in appearance, these cats feel a little weird and greasy to the touch if you're used to, um, cat hair. Be

aware: this breed is not hypoallergenic. The dander found in dried cat saliva, not the fur, is what's causing your allergies—and your Sphynx will still groom himself. Check out "Can I get a hypoallergenic cat?" in this chapter for more information on dander, saliva, and allergies.

It's important to know the basics about each breed, and you can easily find it on the Internet. Carefully research breed information, and when in doubt, stick with reliable sources such as the CFA, which is the world's largest organization of pedigreed cats. This is the equivalent of the dog's American Kennel Club.

How long is my girlfriend's cat going to live?

The average indoor cat lives between fourteen and eighteen years. Some geriatric cats can live up to twenty years of age. Unfortunately, the life span is much shorter for those cats that seek the adventures of the great outdoors, reportedly ranging from two to five years of age.[4] The top causes of death for indoor cats include chronic kidney failure and cancer; for outdoor cats, the main causes include trauma (like being hit by a car, attacked by another animal, shot by the neighborhood brat) and infectious diseases such as feline leukemia, feline infectious peritonitis, or feline immunodeficiency virus. Don't dig your girlfriend's cat? Making him an outdoor weekend warrior is indeed . . . inappropriate!

Recently, an interesting dog study completed by Purina evaluated food-restricted dogs versus control-fed dogs (dogs fed the amount recommended on dog food packages), and found that food-restricted dogs weighed less and had lower body fat content.[5] In this study, the average life span was significantly longer for dogs in which food was restricted. The onset of clinical signs of chronic disease was also delayed for food-restricted dogs. Results suggest that a 25 percent restriction in food intake increased median life span and delayed the onset of signs of chronic disease.[6] In other words, thinner dogs may live longer than obese or overweight dogs, which is important to remember when 40 to 70 percent of America's animals are obese.[7] The reason why we cat owners should care is because we all want our cats to live to their twenties, right? Being that the majority of our housecats are obese, this is encouraging news to help Felix abide by his New Year's resolution. We're still waiting for Purina to do this study in cats, but in general, this advice is probably true for all species (yours and mine included!). In addition to weight loss, annual, routine veterinary care is important, particularly as your cat ages, as it can help detect medical problems sooner.

It's important to realize how long you have to commit to a cat—while that kitten looks adorable in the pet store or humane society, you have to prepare for a twenty-year commitment! That's a lot of kitty litter, 3 A.M. wake-up exercise runs around your head (while you're sleeping), cat food, veterinary bills, and thankfully, purring and loving in return.

Should I dump my boyfriend because he doesn't like my cat?

Yes.

Check out "How do I make my boyfriend like cats?" in chapter 4 for some tidbits, but in the meantime, think long and hard.

What are the top ten hottest cat names?

Based on a 2007 study by Veterinary Pet Insurance (VPI), the top ten cat names are (drum roll, please!):

THE TOP TEN FEMALE CAT NAMES ARE:

1. Chloe
2. Lucy
3. Cleo
4. Princess
5. Angel
6. Molly
7. Kitty (come on, people, let's get some imagination here!)
8. Samantha
9. Misty
10. Missy

THE TOP TEN MALE CAT NAMES ARE:

1. Max
2. Tigger
3. Tiger
4. Smokey
5. Oliver
6. Simba
7. Shadow
8. Buddy
9. Sam
10. Sammy

OF THE 450,000 CATS THAT ARE INSURED BY VPI, THE TOP TEN MOST POPULAR CAT NAMES (COMBINING THE SEXES) ARE:

1. Max
2. Chloe
3. Lucy
4. Tigger

5. Tiger
6. Smokey
7. Oliver
8. Bella
9. Sophie
10. Princess

If you want to avoid being boring, here are a few helpful hints when it comes to picking a name for your new cat. First of all, don't rush to name your new kitten too fast—after all, she'll blow you off for weeks before she'll even pretend to start recognizing her name anyway. Maybe her personality will give you a clue on what to name her. You'll need some time to discover that Crazy is really shy, while Mojo is surprisingly lazy. Personally, I always like to name pets after memories—whether it's my favorite client, patient, city, or hiking spot. I picked the name Seamus because I had a long-term patient with that name while I was living in Boston. Out of humility, I decided to keep that great name when I erroneously called out for "See-mus" (rather than the proper Irish, "Shamus" pronunciation) in the waiting room. One of my colleagues named her new kitten Tettegouche after one of our favorite hiking spots in northern Minnesota. Granted, "Tettegouche" is a mouthful, but Gouche ended up being a really cute nickname.

Next, pick a name that your cat will easily recognize, otherwise all he'll hear is "blah, blah, blah, blah." Using a two-syllable name that ends with a vowel (Monkee, Sallie) may make it easier for your cat to identify his or her new name. One of my clients named her cat Ulysses, but his easier, more recognizable nickname is Fatty. Ends with a vowel, no matter how un–politically correct it is, so I guess it's OK. He seems to recognize it just fine. Finally, pick a name you won't be embarrassed by when your veterinarian hollers it out in the waiting room. "Pussy" is a bit embarrassing for your vet to call out, no matter how funny you may find it.

Is it better to buy a purebred cat or a "mutt" (domesticated short-haired cat)?

In general, I advocate adopting a cat from a shelter or rescue situation unless you are seeking a specific breed for a specific purpose. Don't get me wrong, I have my personal breed biases and would love to own some purebreds. However, with the growing problem of pet overpopulation, you can rescue a plain, old, boring (but lovable) mutt cat from being euthanized in a shelter. In general, because of hybrid vigor, which is the combination of the "best genetic material," domestic short-haired cats are often healthier and have a lower risk for inherited diseases.

More recently, breed-specific rescue groups have evolved. Purebred cats may be surrendered owing to owner issues or because of behavioral or medical problems, and organized breed-specific foster organizations help find homes for these purebred cats. Alternatively, many local animal shelters often have purebred cats available for adoption. Some shelters are even willing to put you on a breed-specific waiting list. It's always best to look around to see what options are available.

How do I pick the right cat from a breeder?

Again, I must extol the benefits of "hybrid vigor" here. Domesticated cats, or "mutts," have fewer problems than do purebred cats, owing to the enhanced genetic pooling of "better" genetic material; plus, you can usually get a "mutt" for free. It's not that domesticated short-haired cats or domesticated long-haired cats never have medical problems; it's just that the incidence is lower.

Health notwithstanding, another good reason to adopt a plain Jane cat is to help reduce pet overpopulation within shelters. There are millions of "unwanted" cats each year in America, and by adopting one, you not only save a life but you also help reduce the number of cats that are euthanized each year because of overpopulation.

All of that said, nothing is wrong with wanting a purebred. Specific breeds really do have wonderful characteristics, and if you are seeking a specific color or coat pattern, then a purebred cat may be just what you are looking for. Whether you want a show cat or just a show-off-to-your-friends cat, purebreds are the best bet when it comes to getting the exact color, make, or model that you want. Before randomly purchasing one, however, make sure to be an educated consumer and do your homework. It's important to obtain previous medical history from the breeder prior to purchasing your purebred. Have the parents or littermates shown signs of inherited, or congenital, diseases seen within that breed? Responsible breeders are those who advocate certification or testing prior to purchase to make sure they are selling healthy cats. Lines of heart disease, asthma, diabetes, or inflammatory bowel disease may also be more predominant, and a thorough lineage and history should be obtained from the breeder before purchase. Be wary of breeders whose entire line of cats are without flaw—this is very unlikely. Responsible breeders will readily provide this information and should be honest. Prevent future heartache by ensuring that your kitten is healthy first by doing your homework.

Next, go visit the breeder and check out the facilities. Are the cage conditions clean, dry, well kept? Do they have good lighting and a good environment? If you are visiting cages in a dark basement or garage, look elsewhere. Are the parents available for you to examine? Have the parents both been well vaccinated and well cared for by a veterinarian with routine annual examinations? Is everyone in the breeding facility negative for feline leukemia and feline immunodeficiency virus? Has the breeder ever had a reported case of feline infectious peritonitis? Are the parents on flea and tick preventative, or, ideally, indoor only? Are the littermates all healthy and cared for? The breeder should have dewormed them and given them their first vaccine (of a series of three to four kitten shots). If this hasn't been done, I recommend that you look elsewhere. If the breeder can't afford that first vaccine and exam, then he or she can't afford to breed and probably shouldn't be. In addition, kittens should ideally stay with their mother until at least six to seven (or ideally, eight) weeks of age to ensure appropriate socialization; anyone selling prior to this age will give their kittens abandonment issues and may not be looking out for the welfare of that cat. Finally, a responsible breeder should be willing to guarantee the health of the kitten for reimbursement or exchange if there are problems detected.

If you aren't sure where to turn to begin your purebred search, get a recommendation from a veterinarian for a good breeder. Ask your friends and family. Do research on the Internet. Be an educated consumer. It's heartbreaking to see clients who have bonded with their kitten only to find out eight weeks later she has a congenital disease. I can pretty much guarantee your new kitten will quickly grow on you, and you want to make sure she's healthy from the start.

Do cats really have nine lives?

Cats have an amazing ability to survive, and that's coming from a vet! I've seen some cats that have survived crazy odds. A colleague's kitten came in to the Animal Medical Center (AMC) in New York City half frozen, barely alive. Despite avid attempts of doing cardiopulmonary cerebral resuscitation, the kitten died and was not able to be revived. Because of another emergency, the doctor rushed off, only to come back to find that the surgery light had been left on and the kitten was now alive, warmed up and revived by the light. Apparently, you're not dead until you're warm and dead. The kitten was bravely named Ripley, after *Ripley's Believe It or Not!* He did sustain some underlying kidney failure from it, but he was the AMC emergency room miracle mascot for several years. So, yes, some cats have nine lives.

How do I pill my cat?

Now, as a cat owner, I can empathize with those poor clients whom I send home with either the liquid or pill form of antibiotics. It's not quite as easy as it looks, and it wasn't until I actually tried giving liquid medication to my own cat that I realized it's harder to give than pills.

Before starting, make sure that you either are holding the pill between the thumb and forefinger of your dominant hand or that it is placed near you, within arm's reach. The easiest way to begin is to position your cat correctly: with his back to you, gently wedge him between your legs as you squat over him. Using your nondominant hand, place your forefinger and your thumb around the cheeks of your cat—safely behind those canine teeth (the large pointy ones) of the upper jaw, so he can't bite you. Simultaneously direct your cat's nose to the ceiling, causing him to slightly open his lower jaw. Place the dominant hand's middle finger between your cat's lower canine teeth and quickly pull down on his bottom jaw as you drop the pill held by your thumb and forefinger into the back of his throat, continuing to keep his nose lifted toward the ceiling. Use gentle pressure to close your cat's mouth while he licks around and (hopefully) swallows the medication. It can also help to gently stroke his throat, which will encourage involuntary swallowing.

If my description doesn't clue you in, don't despair—there are numerous great videos and websites on the Internet that show you how to pill a cat.[8] Check out veterinary sources such as the Cornell Feline Health Center for video tips. When in doubt, ask your veterinarian or technician to show you how to give the first pill. Before you know it, you'll either (a) be a pilling pro or (b) find a bunch of spit-out pills behind the living room sofa.

For those of you experienced cat-medicating owners, here's some food for thought that's been circulating on the Web![9]

How to Pill a Cat

1. Pick up cat and cradle it in the crook of your left arm as if holding a baby. Position right forefinger and thumb on each side of cat's mouth and gently apply pressure to cheeks while holding pill in right hand. As cat opens mouth, pop pill into mouth. Allow cat to close mouth and swallow.

2. Retrieve pill from floor and cat from behind sofa. Cradle cat gently in left arm and repeat process.

3. Retrieve cat from bedroom; pick up and throw away soggy pill.

4. Take new pill from foil wrap, cradle cat in left arm, holding rear paws tightly with left hand. Force jaws open and push pill to back of mouth with right forefinger. Hold mouth shut for count of ten.

5. Retrieve pill from goldfish bowl and cat from top of wardrobe. Call spouse in from garden.

6. Kneel on floor with cat wedged firmly between knees, and hold front and rear paws. Ignore low growls emitted by cat. Get spouse to hold head firmly with one hand while forcing wooden ruler into cat's mouth. Drop pill down ruler and rub cat's throat vigorously.

7. Retrieve cat from curtain rail. Get another pill out of foil wrap. Make note to buy new ruler and repair curtains.

8. Wrap cat in large towel and get spouse to lie on cat with head just visible from below armpit. Put pill in end of drinking straw, force mouth open with a pencil and blow into drinking straw.

9. Check label to make sure pill not harmful to humans, drink glass of water to take taste away. Apply Band-Aid to spouse's forearm and remove blood from carpet with cold water and soap.

10. Retrieve cat from neighbor's shed. Get another pill. Place cat in cupboard and close door just enough so that head is showing. Force mouth open with dessert spoon. Have spouse flick pill down throat with rubber band.

11. Fetch screwdriver from garage and put cupboard door back on hinges. Apply cold compress to cheek and check records for date of last tetanus shot.

12. Get spouse to drive you to emergency room. Sit quietly while doctor stitches fingers and forearms and removes pill from right eye.

13. Arrange for ASPCA to collect cat and contact local pet shop to see if they have any hamsters.

1. Wrap pill in bacon.

As you can tell, it's not as easy as it looks. Ask your vet for some helpful hints (like fish-flavored compounded medication) if you need to!

Why are so many people allergic to cats and what causes these allergies?

We're not sure why it seems like more and more people are allergic to cats recently. Perhaps more owners are keeping their cats indoors for the felines' health and safety, so the allergens are more prominent. It could also be that cats have topped dogs in overall popularity, and with almost 80 million cats in homes it could be that more people are now discovering that they are allergic. Unfortunately, the culprit is Fel d 1, a glycoprotein that cats naturally produce and secrete from their sebaceous glands and then shed in the skin and saliva. As cats groom themselves, they shed this allergen all over their body (and your house, carpet, bed, linens, and clothes), triggering your red, itchy eyes and runny nose.

Can I get a hypoallergenic cat?

Voted as one of *Time* magazine's 2006 best medical inventions, the hypoallergenic cat from Allerca Lifestyle Pets can be yours for as little as $5,950 or as much as $125,000. Apparently, Lifestyle Pets has found a way to create genetic divergences (which they call the Allerca GD cat) that minimize the cat allergen Fel d 1, creating a cat that won't trigger your allergies. Depending on how "exotic" you want your new hypoallergenic cat to be (perhaps with some African Serval or Asian Leopard Cat blended in), you may be paying up to

$125,000. Don't worry—these hypoallergenic cats are supposed to be "friendly, playful, and affectionate,"[10] although for all that money they should be able to scoop their own litter box and bring in your mail while they're at it. For all that money, you can pick a medium-length hair coat, an assortment of coat colors and patterns, and even different-sized cats. Of course, there's a one- to two-year waiting list, but if you pay an extra $1,950, you can reduce your wait from two years to just a few months.

See, money may be able to buy you happiness, after all. Or a lot of Kleenex and Claritin.

I love my cat, but I'm so allergic! What should I do?

For those of you who are allergic to your cat, don't believe your cat-hating medical doctor—you don't *necessarily* have to get rid of your cat just because you have allergies. Of course, if you have severe allergies and asthma, and medications just aren't working for you, that may be a different story. Typically, avoidance is the best preventative medicine for your allergies, but cats are just so lovely, we can't survive without their existence (much to our allergist's dismay). There are a surprisingly high percentage of veterinarians with cat allergies too, but we just deal with it by avoiding cat-sniffing contests and by taking antihistamines. Thankfully, I'm not allergic to anything but rabbits, so I avoid bun-buns like the plague.

There are a few tricks of the trade that you can do to minimize the severity of your allergies. With the use of high-efficiency particulate air (HEPA) filters, antihistamines, inhalers, steroids, and allergy shots, some mild forms of allergies are manageable. That said, please consult your medical doctor or allergist for the right antihistamine for long-term use. Having hardwood floors that are easier to clean than carpets can help, and vacuuming frequently (with a HEPA filter in the vacuum) can also relieve some symptoms. Keeping a cat-free area in your house, reserved just for you two-legged types, is also important (for example, the bedroom, where you spend a third of your life). Lastly, even though your cat will hate you, simply washing him with water once a week will dramatically remove the amount of dander (which is all over his skin and fur as he's licking and grooming everywhere). If you're financially gifted, or can afford to wait two years, a hypoallergenic cat is always another option.

Do I have to get rid of my cat because my kids are allergic?

For any pediatric allergists reading this, don't make your patients get rid of their cat just because their child has allergies! Studies have shown that the younger the infant is exposed to allergens such as cat dander and dog fur, the *fewer* allergies they have as adults.[11] Of course, if your cat is triggering asthmatic, allergic attacks in your children, then you should have a heart-to-heart with your husband on whether or not to get rid of the cat or the kid.

How can I make my own cat more tolerable for guests with allergies?

If you happen to have a lot of friends with cat allergies, make sure to run a HEPA (high-efficiency particulate air) filter for a few days prior to having those friends over (guess this rules out surprise drop-bys). A thorough vacuuming and deep cleaning of your house before their arrival will also help. Actually, ripping up your carpets permanently and replacing them with hardwood floors will help the most . . . but I guess that depends on how "close" a friend they really are. Provided you have a good air filter that you're replacing often, running the

AC or furnace will also help remove some of the dander. If your friends drop by, keep your cats in a room no one will be using, so your guests aren't directly exposed to your cats. Lastly, consider giving out Claritin as party favors. Your last desperate option is to only be friends with nonallergic cat lovers.

Why do a cat's rear-limb nails seem to grow slower than the forelimb nails?

Most cat owners notice that they rarely have to cut their cat's hind-limb nails, while the forelimb nails grow at a much faster rate. Why is this? Well, we're not really sure—there's no pathophysiological reason why this happens. Cats normally use their forelimb nails for defense, climbing, and digging in the litter box, so they end up potentially shredding their nails and wearing them down more frequently. This may stimulate them to grow faster and faster. Rear-limb nails are used to help boost cats up a tree and to help attack or "play" with another housemate by "rabbit kicking" them with their back legs, but these nails don't really pose too much more function. We suspect that because cats use their forelimb nails so much more frequently, they grow more quickly to stay razor sharp.

How do I cut my cat's nails and how often do I have to do it?

Ah, the joy of cat ownership. It's not always as easy as it looks, right? Not only do you have to clean your cat's litter box while allowing him to poop in your house, but you also have to attempt to cut his nails while avoiding an emergency room visit (for you!) in the process. The best way to cut your cat's nails is to train him early so you don't get mauled in the process. When your cat is still a kitten, gently play with his or her toes and paw pads for a few seconds or minutes a day—that way, he'll get use to you touching his feet (after all, not all of us have foot fetishes). Second, use a gentle, effective nail trimmer. I personally prefer the miniature black rubber-handled cat nail clippers that look like scissors. They are small, easy to handle, inexpensive, and well worth it. Human fingernail trimmers also work well, as they are sleek and small. Don't even think about using those bulky, cold, metal guillotine dog clippers—those will shred your cat's nails, and he'll be stuck with a painful and ugly manicure!

Next, remember to be patient. Don't bother trying to clip all the nails in one sitting; both you and your cat will hate each other. I clip one foot at a time, and accept what I can get from my cats. Your cat might be wondering why he's tap dancing with his long nails on one foot, and flat-footed on the other, but trust me—he prefers this over a whole body tackle-and-torture session.

When trimming your cat's nails, place your thumb on the top of the digit and your forefinger on the bottom pad. Push them both together gently, and you'll notice that the nail extends out, so you can see more of it. You'll notice a clear and pink part, and you want to quickly and efficiently trim as much of the clear part off as you can in one swipe. Don't go too close to the pink tissue (the quick, where the nerve and blood vessels run), as this is painful and will bleed. After tackling a few trims, give your cat a much-deserved treat and yourself a break.

How often you clip your cat's nails depends on how much you like your leather sofa. I try to remember to do it once a month, and get painfully reminded to do it when Seamus and Echo walk over my head at 3 A.M. trying to snuggle with me. Because the front nails seem to grow faster than the hind nails, you'll find that you'll have to cut the back ones with less frequency (which is a good thing, since it's more awkward and difficult to cut back nails). I find that I have to cut my cats' front nails once a month, but the back ones every few months. That said, when in doubt, it's always safest to keep your cat's nails trimmed as short as possible, so no one gets hurt (i.e., you!). This is particularly important if you have children or other pets in the household, as you want to avoid any scratches or injuries (intentional or not). Remember, the sharper the cat nail, the more severe the potential for injury (as it can cut deeper into the tissue). Also, there are some rare diseases you can catch from your cat scratching you, so you want to keep those nails trim (see "What is cat scratch fever?" in chapter 10 for more information).

If your cat has hyperthyroidism (a condition in which the thyroid gland is overactive), you may notice your cat's nails growing at an abnormally rapid rate. The nails often become more brittle and very thick, and can crack while you cut them. While your cat doesn't need a paraffin wax manicure or Vaseline Intensive Care, just be careful when cutting the nails. More important, if you simultaneously notice signs of excessive drinking, bigger clumps in the litter box, and weight loss despite a ravenous appetite, bring your cat to a vet for a thyroid check—and a free nail trim while she's at it. See "What's hyperthyroidism?" in this chapter for more information.

Why does my cat use my couch as a scratching post and how do I make him stop?

Despite the hundreds of dollars you spend buying cute little cat carpet condos, scratching posts, catnip, and toys for your cat, he somehow prefers the more expensive items like your microfiber sofa. Why?

Cats scratch for several reasons. Because cats have scent glands under their paw pads, they like to spread the love around and make sure that other cats know that this part of the house is theirs. Cats also scratch because it feels good—you may have let their nails grow too long, and it's their way of naturally wearing down their nails or ripping them off in the process (did you ever notice that you find the occasional outer layer of the toenail lying around?). Scratching also feels great—it stretches their front limbs and is almost the equivalent of our getting a hand massage.

There are a few things you can do to prevent your cat from scratching. First, keep your cat's nails short, as it'll cause less damage and will hopefully minimize the urge to scratch. Second, try making your furniture less appealing to the touch (as microfiber is just so soft). You can do this by applying double-sided tape or aluminum foil to the scratched area—just make sure the tape doesn't damage your furniture worse than your cat would (clue: don't apply duct tape to antique wood). The sticky feel of double-sided tape on the affected area will quickly fend off any feline fingers. If you want to attract some really strange looks from your houseguests, tape aluminum foil to your furniture—that cold, metallic, crinkling touch will send your cat running away! Soon your cat will quickly learn that the sofa's scratching surface isn't quite as fun and appealing as it used to be. Of course, your friends will think your decor is a bit strange, but hey, anything to save the microfiber. The bad news is that as soon as you take away the tape or foil, your cat may be right back at it with a vengeance. One furniture hint: my postmatriculation gift to myself was an expensive Italian leather sofa set (that came with a five-year warranty); the salesman assured me that the leather was pliable and soft enough to yield to the pressure of animal nails, and he was right. The leather material just doesn't attract my cats, and knock on wood, I have no scratch marks on it as of yet.

Another way of curbing your cat's couch habits is to use negative feedback. With this technique, you have to actually *catch* your cat in the act. If you do, a quick blast of water from a water gun will quickly teach him not to scratch in front of you. Of course, your cat may scratch all day long while you're at work, but at least it'll make you feel like the alpha cat for a few minutes. Unfortunately, it's unlikely your cat will learn to restrain himself in your absence, and unless you plan on quitting your job to protect your sofa, you may need to resort to other options.

Last and most important, train your cat to use the right kind of scratching posts. If your cheap two-dollar scratching post is hidden in the dark, dank corner of the basement where nobody wants to go, it's not going to be effective. If the material doesn't feel good to scratch (i.e., cheap cardboard), your cat won't use it. Only the best for your cat! Try twine, coarse rope, carpet, or sisal (a type of material that looks like carpet), and make sure the post is well placed and well constructed (if it falls on top of your cat while he's scratching, I can guarantee you he'll never use it again). Although it may affect your feng shui, keep the scratching post in the center of the room or next to the vertical or horizontal surface your cat scratches, as cats always prefer to be the center of attention. I have one of my scratching posts under the coffee table; it's not glaringly offensive to those interior decorator friends who visit, but it's in a central enough location where my cats will use it.

Finally, try bribery. Entice your cat to play around the post by placing treats or toys there. You can always sprinkle catnip on the surface of the scratching posts, as chemical persuasion is OK under certain circumstances, right? If all else fails, you can consult a veterinary behaviorist, or, worst-case scenario, consider declawing. I personally don't perform this surgical procedure, but if it means your not surrendering your cat to the humane society or (even worse), euthanizing your cat, then I support your decision.

Is declawing cats cruel?

The debate to declaw cats is an ongoing discussion even among veterinarians. Some veterinarians advocate declawing for two reasons. First, it may help a cat get adopted as it reduces the risk of damaging furniture. Second, it may prevent some cats from being humanely euthanized owing to furniture damage or scratching children in the house.

In general, I'm a fan of trying behavioral modification, training, and prevention instead of declawing. I personally don't declaw. Sure, I've learned the procedure and have done it once or twice in veterinary school, but I'm no expert at it. That's because I completed my internship at Angell Memorial Animal Hospital (associated with the Massachusetts Society for the Prevention of Cruelty to Animals), where the procedure wasn't performed on ethical grounds.

If the tricks of the trade (like behavioral modification and training) don't work and your cat is blowing you off, he or she may need to be declawed. First, know that there are many different options for declawing: onychectomy, laser therapy, tendonectomy, and the use of Soft Paws. Generally, when veterinarians declaw, they typically only do the front toenails, as these are the nails that rip up your sofa. While it's less expensive to only declaw the forelimbs, please know that declawing the back leg nails is generally unnecessary and probably putting your cat through more pain than necessary. Keep in mind that if you have your cat's front paws declawed, you still have to remember to trim those back-leg nails every few months.

Onychectomy is removing the third digital phalanx with a scalpel or nail clipper. This removes the last part of your cat's digit (i.e., the top third of your finger with the nail on it), and should prevent nails from ever growing back. This is the most common type of declawing available from your veterinarian and generally goes off without a hitch. Occasional complications from this method include pain, bleeding, pad damage, transient paw swelling, infection, or chronic lameness. Rarely, incomplete removal of the germinal cells during the procedure can cause the nail to grow back. Because this type of declawing is the most painful method, make sure your vet is treating your brave kitty with lots of pain medication both before and after surgery.

Laser therapy is another method of nonsurgical onychectomy. Laser therapy is quick, causes minimal tissue injury, and results in rapid healing. However, not a lot of veterinarians have this expensive gadget, so there's limited availability. Also, the use of laser therapy is dependent on the experience of the veterinarian, so be sure to consult with your vet to see if this is an option.

Deep digital flexor tendonectomy is less invasive, as the actual nail is not removed. Rather, the tendon in the wrist is cut, making it impossible for your cat to protract his nails. In other words, he has his loaded gun but can't whip it out. The claws remain retracted after these tendons are severed, which limits the ability to scratch, but the nails may become blunt and thick, and will still need to be trimmed regularly. With tendonectomy, rare complications can occur. For example, if your vet accidentally cuts the wrong tendon (the adjacent superficial digital flexor tendon), your cat may have a permanent, abnormal flat-footed stance. The good news is that he can't be drafted.

In general, if you're going to get your cat declawed, do it sooner rather than later (around three to six months of age). You want to do it before your cat learns to scratch furniture. More important, do it sooner because young cats recover and heal faster—they are back to playing and running within days. Despite the urban myth, declawing older cats doesn't screw up their balance and agility, but their recovery can take a few weeks longer. Finally, find a veterinarian who uses pain medication after surgery. I always like to send cats home on an oral pain medication, Buprenex (a morphine-like drug), for several days after any kind of surgery.

For those of you who are scared or nervous about surgery, a nonsurgical option includes Soft Paws. These are vinyl caps that you glue to your cat's front claws and are a noninvasive way of attempting to prevent your cat from damaging furniture. While it may not be comfortable (imagine typing with fake nails), cats seem to tolerate them reasonably well. The Soft Paws website also provides useful tips on how to cut your cat's nails, how to fill the caps with adhesive, and how to adhere them to your cat quickly and safely (see Resources). Supposedly, Soft Paws stick on for four to six weeks (depending on your skill in gluing), but I randomly found them throughout the house, in the litter box, and in Seamus's poop (they're pretty safe and are supposedly easy to pass, as Seamus proved) when I tried them. The good thing is that it lets you try on all the different colors and styles in the process. And no, you can't drop your cat off at your manicurist to have this done, but you will become a pro at it after your first ten or twelve Soft Paws get stuck to your hair, your cat's face, your fingertips, and your clothes.

Can I let my declawed cat outside?

Letting a declawed cat outdoors is like letting him go to battle without a gun. Because cats can't protect themselves without their nails, they should be kept indoors once declawed. If your declawed cat is craving to go outdoors, consider supervising Kitty outside while using a leash (see "Can

I train my cat to walk on a leash or body harness?" in chapter 5). While some declawed cats can still climb trees to escape danger (by using their hind-limb nails), it's obviously more difficult and puts your cat in immediate danger. I've seen too many cats in the emergency room that have been fatally mauled by dogs or coyotes, and when I see that they're poor, defenseless, declawed cats that have been let outdoors, I'm left feeling frustrated and heartbroken.

Why does my cat have extra toes?

Just like the rare human who has extra fingers, cats can have extra toes. Polydactylism is a condition that results in an extra nubbin—which may or may not be functional—and may not have normal bone or joint development. While this inherited trait doesn't help your cat (he still won't be able to pick up a pencil), it doesn't hurt him either. In Ithaca, New York, a particular orange and white male tabby tomcat with extra toes seemed to get around town a lot, and as a result, Ithaca has a noticeably higher rate of feline polydactyly. While this isn't a medical problem, don't forget to cut the nails on that extra toe. Seamus, my gray and white tabby that I adopted in Boston, has two extra toes on each forelimb; in fact, I almost named him Fenway since he has such huge mitts. Unfortunately, the Red Sox weren't doing too well back then, so I elected not to. Now I regret it.

Can my cat donate blood?

Believe it or not, we do blood transfusions in veterinary medicine too. Cats that lose blood from surgery or develop anemia (from kidney failure, immune problems, cancer, or feline leukemia) may need a blood transfusion to boost their red blood cell count. Cats have only three main blood types:

A, B, and AB. OK, there is one other new blood type called Mik (named after a cat named Michael), but this type is so rare that there's not a good test for it yet. That said, all cats need to be blood typed (which can be done simply by running a blood test) before getting a transfusion, as there is no "universal donor" in cats (they can't take your O-negative blood).

If you live near a veterinary school or large specialty referral hospital, consider having your cat become a periodic blood donor. Not only will Kitty get a gold star from her veterinarian, but she'll also get free cat food, a physical exam, and good cat karma for the future. Because cats aren't quite as laid back as dogs, they do need to be sedated for blood donation, no matter how good their veins are. In general, cats have to be fairly friendly, weigh over ten pounds (that's lean body weight, not fat, mind you), be between two and seven years of age, current on vaccinations, healthy with a normal physical exam, not receiving any medications (other than heartworm, flea, and tick preventative), and indoor only (and that includes all the companion housemate cats too). Cats also have to test negative for feline leukemia and feline immunodeficiency virus, must never have been previously bred, and never have been previously transfused. While that sounds like a long list, see if your cat qualifies, as she can help save another kitty's life. It's a very rewarding feeling!

What are FIV and FeLV?

Kitty AIDS is known as feline immunodeficiency virus (FIV) and is caused by a lentivirus, which is in the same family of retroviruses similar to feline leukemia (FeLV). While these two cat viruses *cannot* be transmitted to humans, they are both similar to human AIDS and were the primary viruses researchers used to first study the AIDS virus in humans. Both FIV and FeLV can be transmitted to other cats by saliva, blood, and bodily fluids, although the most common ways are from fighting (with that neighborhood stray) or through the placenta (from mother to kitten). These viruses can also be transmitted by sexual contact, though this is rare. Aggressive, intact (unneutered), outdoor male cats who like to bite and fight are usually the most predisposed to these viruses and spread these viruses along through biting. That said, if you let your healthy cat outside, check out "Should I get my cat vaccinated for feline leukemia?" in chapter 10.

Cats can live with FIV for much longer than those cats with FeLV, although both viruses are similar to HIV and act by suppressing a cat's immune system, causing chronic illness, malaise, and weight loss. Affected cats can't fight off bacteria, viruses, and parasites that a normal cat can fight off, resulting in anemia, severe gum disease, fever, eye problems (uveitis), difficulty breathing (from fluid around the lungs), and even cancer (lymphosarcoma).

Being that these potentially fatal viruses can dramatically shorten the life span of your newly adopted kitten or, even worse, be spread to your other housecats, it's important to test your new adoptee as soon as possible. Your veterinarian can test your new kitten immediately with just a few drops of blood and will find out the results within minutes. Thankfully, the blood test is pretty accurate, so you can rest assured once you get home. If however, your cat tests positive, consult with your veterinarian on what is best to do. Unfortunately, because both viruses are so contagious to other cats, positive-testing cats should be kept indoors only in a one-cat home or with other FeLV- or FIV-positive cats. After all, you don't want your infectious cat to be the Typhoid Mary of the 'hood, do you?

What's hyperthyroidism?

Hyperthyroidism, a hormone (or endocrine, for those of you who want to sound scientifically gifted) disorder, is when the thyroid gland produces too much thyroid hormone. This results in an overstimulated, hyperactive metabolism. Typically, the thyroid glands lie on both sides of the trachea, and we veterinarians normally shouldn't be able to feel them (which is probably why you astute cat owners wonder why we're trying to manhandle your cat's neck during your cat's routine vet exam). If we palpate a thyroid nodule, rest assured—it's rarely cancerous. That said, we're worried it's a benign but overactive "adenoma" (which produces excessive hormone tissue), which can eventually lead to hyperthyroidism. Keep in mind that if your veterinarian detects an early adenoma, it may not be "functional" yet. In other words, yes, your cat will *eventually* become hyperthyroid at some point but may not be now. I freaked out a year ago because I found a thyroid nodule on Seamus. Thankfully, he had a normal blood thyroid level and wasn't showing any symptoms yet. Unfortunately, this thyroid nodule is likely to become active one of these years, so I'll have to keep a close eye on it.

Typically, cats develop hyperthyroidism in their middle-aged to geriatric years. If you notice your cat losing weight, drinking more than usual, urinating larger clumps in the litter box, vomiting more than normal, or eating ravenously despite weight loss (don't we all wish we had that problem), then take your cat to a veterinarian for blood work and a thyroid test. Don't worry—it's not fatal, but it does need to be treated, or severe life-threatening side effects like high blood pressure, heart disease, and blindness can occur. Talk to your veterinarian about all your options, which include oral medications (methimazole), radioactive iodine treatment (I_{131}), surgery, or even chemical ablation.

Are cats with white fur and blue eyes deaf?

Deafness in white cats with blue eyes was detected as early as 1828[12] and was documented in Darwin's *The Origin of Species* in 1859. Almost forty years later, blue-eyed Dalmatians were reported to be deaf. Since then, there has been more definitive proof of the correlation between white pigmentation, blue eyes, and deafness in dogs and cats.[13] While complex, this correlation is likely due to melanocytes, which are the cells responsible for the pigmentation of skin and hair. These cells originate from the neural crest, which is the source of all neural (or nerve) cells in the embryo. As boring as this sounds, this explains the origin of the link between pigmentation and neurological problems.

I won't overwhelm you with the explanation of pigment granules in melanocytes and abnormal neural crest cell migration, but geneticists have shown that some (but not all) animals with white fur and blue eyes are deaf. Because there is some variation in the expression of genes (or the ability of a gene to express its trait), a modest percentage of white cats with blue eyes may be deaf. If your white cat has smudges of dark, some degree of black, or one different-colored eye (i.e., one blue eye, one green), you may be in luck, as these variables mean your cat is less likely to be deaf due to this complex genetic link.

If you're not sure if your cat is deaf, try behavior-testing your cat at home before you come in for an official veterinary exam. Does Whitey respond to your shaking a Pounce container? If not, you can take your cat in for a BAER (brainstem auditory evoked response) hearing test at your local veterinary neurologist. If you do happen to discover that your blue-eyed, white cat is deaf, fear not. Most cats ignore what you say anyway, so rest assured that Whitey will just *always* blow off your voice. Luckily, deaf cats quickly adapt to their handicap and utilize other senses such as vision, stimuli from their whiskers (from air movement), and vibrations to help compensate. Unfortunately, lifestyle changes have to occur if you own a deaf cat—please don't let him outside, as Whitey won't be able to hear that barking dog or that stalking squirrel. Otherwise, he's pretty content to eat, sleep, poop, and ignore you the rest of the time.

What does it mean when my cat starts losing weight?

The top four causes of weight loss in cats are chronic kidney (renal) failure, diabetes, hyperthyroidism, and cancer. With the first three diseases, you may notice that your cat is drinking more than usual. If you even *think* your cat is drinking too much water, trust me, he is and it's been going on longer than you think.

If you notice you're going through more and more kitty litter, your cat is sitting by the water bowl, or you're scooping out larger and larger clumps of urine, cowboy up and bring your cat to a veterinarian for a physical examination and some testing. Your veterinarian will want to perform an exam on your cat to feel the intestines, stomach, kidneys, and thyroid. Blood tests should include doing a routine chemistry panel (which evaluates the liver and kidney function, protein, blood glucose/sugar, and electrolytes), a complete blood count (which evaluates the red and white blood cells, protein, and platelets), a urinalysis (to see if the urine is too dilute, or if bacteria or crystals are present), and a thyroid test (more commonly called a T_4). If these tests are normal, chest and abdominal x-rays or even an ultrasound may be necessary to find out why your cat is continuing to lose weight. Some of these causes are more easily treatable sooner than later, so don't wait too long to find out what's causing a problem in your beloved furry friend.

Why do cats puke so much?

A few years ago, my housemate (who was an internal medicine resident fascinated by vomit and diarrhea and such) asked me if I ever did blood work and x-rays to find out why Seamus was a chronic vomiter ("What are you talking about? Once a month is *totally* normal for a cat. Whatever!"). After my housemate made me feel guilty, I've pondered why we cat owners are so tolerant of cat vomit. I mean, if *you* vomited once a week for years, wouldn't you go to a medical doctor? If your dog vomited once a week all his life, chances are you'd take him to a veterinarian sooner than later. So why is it that we cat owners tolerate cat puke so much more? Maybe we're blaming frequent vomiting on hair balls, but if your cat is puking that often and there isn't any *hair* in the puke, think again. There may actually be a medical cause for all that vomit.

If your cat is vomiting up hair balls, you'll see Kitty actively retching (with her stomach heaving) and having what we vets grossly call a *productive* vomit. In other words, she'll bring up some bile (yellow-tinged fluid), undigested food, or hair. That said, retching or vomiting can also mimic other problems, such as something stuck in the mouth, throat, or esophagus. If the vomit is nonproductive (i.e., nothing comes out), your cat may be coughing instead, which is a classic sign of asthma. Regardless, if you find your cat doing *either* more than once or twice a month, something more serious may be going on that warrants a trip to the veterinarian. Chest and abdominal x-rays, some basic blood work, and a sterile lung fluid wash (also called an endotracheal lavage) should be done to rule out asthma. Before you blame Kitty for ruining your Persian carpet, make sure you aren't missing a medical problem!

Why do cats get hair balls and why do they look like poop?

Cats are extremely fastidious when it comes to cleanliness and would never be caught dead rolling in foul, decaying carcasses or eating another animal's poop, the way undignified dogs do. Because cats don't usually get quite as dirty as dogs, and because cats dislike water, they don't require (or want) baths. However, since cats can't brush themselves, they groom with their tongue. For those of you who have been French-kissed by the feline species, you realize that their sandpaper-like tongue is quite rough, as it contains tiny fibrous barbs. This helps keep them clean, well groomed, and free of parasites. Unfortunately, they end up swallowing all that hair as a result of their grooming. Because hair digests slowly, it can either pass down the intestinal tract (with the occasional risk of becoming obstructed in the stomach or intestines, requiring surgery), or irritate the stomach, resulting in the 4 A.M. retch as you try to jump out of bed, trip over your light, bang your toe, and catch the vomit on yesterday's newspaper before your cat throws up all over your rug. ("There's just so much hardwood floor everywhere else— why must you only find the carpet?")

Most of the time, hair balls can be managed easily at home. Initially, you can try grooming (bye-bye, fur; helloooo, lion cut!) and brushing (seriously—more than once a week!), along with occasional remedies such as hair-ball-specific food (which has a higher fiber content) or Laxatone, a tasty gel laxative "lubricant," which may help decrease the incidence of hair balls. If that doesn't work, your cat may need a veterinary check to make sure nothing else is going on (like inflammatory bowel disease, kidney failure, parasites, something stuck in the intestines, or even cancer).

Now that we know how to help prevent and treat hair balls,

I'll answer the all-important gross hair ball question: why do hair balls look like poop? As disgusting and gut-wrenching as it sounds, your cat's loud, powerful retching and vomiting can't actually make *feces* come out of her esophagus (it'd have to travel several feet backward through the large and small intestine). So while your cat's hair balls *look* like poop, rest assured that they're *not* poop. What you're picking up is just a tube-shaped hair ball that's been consolidated and smooshed into the shape of your cat's esophagus or stomach.

Why do cats lick down there?

We all know that dogs like to lick their balls and there's no smart excuse for it—it's just because they can reach them. Cats, on the other hand, don't usually do this just for entertainment value. When you see cats licking down there, chances are it's because they're being hygienic.

When you notice that Tigger is contorting himself into a yoga position that your instructor would be proud of, he's actually grooming. Since he can't use toilet paper, and since you don't want to wipe for him, it's all he can do to stay spotless. That said, if Tigger's spending just a bit *too* much time down there, take a closer look, but please don't touch (cats don't like even *gentle* touches). If his penis is sticking out, then something's wrong (see "How come I never see my cat's penis?" in chapter 9). If you notice excessive grooming, lethargy, crying out, bloody urine, inability to urinate for more than twelve to eighteen hours, making multiple trips to the litter box with no obvious urine clumps in there, vomiting, straining, howling, acting as if in pain, or squatting to urinate in strange places (like in your tub, on your comforter, or in your large potted plant—"Hello! What do I have to do to get you to take me to a vet?"), see your veterinarian immediately. Tigger's doing all he can to make you realize he needs help.

He may have a life-threatening feline urethral obstruction (FUO), which is a urinary (bladder) obstruction or blockage. You can imagine how painful it would be not to be able to urinate for a day or two, but more important, having a FUO can cause Tigger to go into kidney failure or die from severe electrolyte abnormalities from not being able to urinate.

Some benign causes for excessive licking "down there" include irritation to Tigger's penis tip, a bladder or urethral (the tube from the bladder to the tip of the penis) stone, or even a sterile cystitis. This last one is also called feline lower urinary tract disease (FLUTD), and is described next. Signs of an FUO are very similar to FLUTD, so when in doubt, bring Tigger to a vet to cop a feel of the bladder—it's the safest and easiest way to make sure Tigger stays happy and healthy!

What is FLUTD and how do I treat it?

Feline lower urinary tract disease (FLUTD), formerly called feline urologic syndrome, is when Tigger *acts* like he has a urinary tract infection (UTI) but really doesn't. Just like when we get a UTI, we always *feel* like we have to urinate every few minutes, even though our bladder is empty. With FLUTD, a sterile inflammation of the bladder causes Tigger to squat, make multiple trips to the litter box, and act like he constantly has to urinate. With FLUTD, antibiotics aren't usually necessary or of benefit, as only 2 percent of FLUTD cases are actually the result of a bacterial UTI. If that's the case, how do we treat it, then?

First, the most important thing to do is to make sure Tigger doesn't have a feline urethral obstruction. After you and your vet have determined that, treatment for FLUTD mostly includes increasing the amount of water that Tigger drinks. Of all the veterinary studies that have been done out there on FLUTD, this is what has been found to help the most—this extra water helps flush out his kidneys and his bladder, relieving some of the inflammation down there. Veterinarians can increase water by giving Tigger some subcutaneous fluids (you know, that big pocket of fluids we give him under the skin?); this will slowly absorb to help hydrate him and flush out his bladder. Second, we recommend feeding canned food (which contains 70 percent water) during these FLUTD crises. I often recommend grueling down the canned food with a few extra teaspoons of water to further increase Tigger's water intake. Next, consider adding a kitty water fountain (see "Why do cats prefer to drink running water?" in chapter 1) to encourage Tigger to drink even more water. Most important, maintain good kitty litter box habits (see "How often do I *really* need to clean my cat's litter box?" in chapter 3). You should be cleaning at least every other day (regardless of how many cats you have) to make sure that Tigger's litter box habits are normal. If you don't check, you won't know!

Some people also associate stress with the development of FLUTD in cats. If you have a stressful environment for your cat (not enough litter boxes, dirty litter boxes, group feeding bowls, lots of transition, or intercat strife), you may be worsening Tigger's symptoms. Try minimizing some of the stress (note to self: heed own advice) and see if that helps. Finally, some studies have looked at using glucosamine (a cartilage protector),[14] pain medications, anti-inflammatories (i.e., meloxicam), and even kitty Prozac, but nothing has been proven to work better than just lots of water.

Can my cat get acne?

Ugh. Remember that awkward, zit-covered juvenile stage that none of us want to repeat? You're feeling ugly, so you stress out, and then bam! Even more zits! Dogs are lucky;

they never have to experience them. Cats, however, do get *feline acne* (the official scientific term for cat zits) under their chin periodically, regardless of how old they are. Feline acne is unrelated to chocolate, hormones, or stress, but know that you can easily treat them with some Stridex pads. Seriously. It's safe—just give Zitty the Kitty a little chin rub. Avoid any other zit creams; only Stridex can safely be applied. If the zits still don't go away, consider consulting a veterinary dermatologist.

Chapter 3
FANCY FELINE

CAT *Fancy* isn't the name of the number-one-selling cat magazine for no reason. As all cat enthusiasts know, our furry feline friends are swanky and act and walk like they know it. While not all of us may own that perfectly groomed, beautifully coated Persian seen in Fancy Feast commercials, we all know that cats strut their stuff for a reason. After all, while it's a dog's life for those drooling types, we're all about the cat's meow.

In this chapter, you'll find out how to spoil your cat rotten. Will the Four Seasons or Fairmont let your cat into your room? Can you take her on vacation with you? Should you fly your cat on a plane when traveling for the weekend? Find out how you can spoil your kitty, what the best colors of nail polish are (OK, Soft Paws), and if she can get her hair dyed and cut while you wait. While you may be spending moola spoiling your cat, know how much you should also save up in a "cat fund" and whether or not to get pet insurance.

At the same time, cats aren't as posh and high-class as you think—there's a dirty part of cat ownership too—it's called *poop*! What's the best way to scoop poop and keep your litter box clean? How often do you *really* need to scoop? These are important things to know, as your veterinarian assumes you already know how to keep your cat's litter box fresh. Whether you're pampering or poop scooping, make sure that you coddle your cat!

In an attempt to spoil my cats rotten, I figured it'd be fun to grow some fresh catnip for Seamus and Echo one summer. Little did I know I was actually supposed to research catnip prior to planting it into my garden. I mean, nobody ever told me that catnip is part of the mint family and highly *invasive*. Planting fresh mint and catnip at the same time was a bad idea—I ended up having a fifth of my garden taken over by these species. I was casually talking to my gardening colleague on the phone when I told her my garden was going gangbusters, particularly my mint and catnip. She gasped and told me that one only plants mint and catnip directly into pots, so they don't spread all over the yard. D'oh.

The good news is that I immediately started pulling up my catnip, which had sent long runners through the dirt in the garden (several feet away). I pulled up about two bushels' worth, dried it in my garage (my neighbors were suspicious, but I promised them it was catnip), and gave it as little stocking stuffers to all my colleagues in the veterinary hospital in small dime bags. ("I swear. It's catnip. Otherwise I'd charge you for it.") I then proceeded to drink a lot of mint mojitos that summer, while my cats enjoyed a lot of euphoria; I pulled up the remaining plants shortly thereafter. The bad news is the mint and catnip both grew back with a vengeance the following season (they can even survive Minnesota winters), but I think I've since gotten it under control (thank you, Roundup!). So if you plan on growing some fresh catnip for your fancy feline friends, go for it. Just put it in pots and not directly into the garden, unless you plan on harvesting acres and acres of it. Read on to find out *safe* ways of spoiling your cat.

How much is this cat going to cost me?

When it comes to pet ownership, it's important to remember that loving and caring for your cat requires more than the $100 that you paid for it at the shelter in adoption fees. Don't get sticker shock *after* you adopt that cute kitten, since now you're fully committed. You'll have to commit to one or two kitty litter boxes ($25), kitty litter ($150/year), cat toys ($30), a scratching post ($100), food ($100/year), water bowls ($20), kitten shots ($75), an annual exam ($50/year) for the next fifteen years ($750), vet bills (gazillions/lifetime), flea preventative ($50/year)—get the hint? Sound like a Master-Card commercial? Costs are minimal when spread out over a decade or so, with all that loving companionship in return, but it's important to be cognizant of your financial responsibility when you rescue that kitten (priceless). When in doubt, check out some websites out there that help you calculate the cost of your cat,[1] and start saving up and investing in the meantime.

Should I get pet insurance for my cat?

Not sure if you should get pet insurance for your cat? Not sure if it's a tried-and-true thing? Well, rest assured, pet insurance has been around for almost thirty years, and over the past decade, it's gotten even more popular. With the improvement in veterinary medical care (now your cat can really get a CAT scan), the costs of health care have gotten progressively more expensive, increasing the costs of pet ownership.

While there are numerous pet insurance companies out there, the top two are Banfield and Veterinary Pet Insurance. Recently, veterinary pet insurance has become progressively more accepted by pet owners, although only about 1 percent of the pet-owning population has it. Considering 30 to 40 percent of Americans lack their own health insurance, this isn't all that surprising.

When you consider the overall costs of pet ownership, pet insurance really isn't that expensive. On average, it costs approximately $1 a day, and if you have multiple pets there's typically a 5 to 10 percent discount for each additional pet. Pet insurance is also accepted everywhere—that's because pet insurance companies are third-party insurers, which means you have to pay your veterinarian up front and seek reimbursement later from your insurance company. That leaves the veterinarians and vet hospitals out of the messy middle (which we prefer).

While some veterinarians do recommend pet insurance, it is important to carefully review your policy. Some companies will only cover a portion of routine vaccines and elective surgeries but will not cover your cat for congenital or inherited diseases. In other words, if your cat's breed is predisposed to heart problems (as is the Maine Coon cat), none of the related medical procedures may be covered. However, pet insurance is helpful in an emergency situation, particularly if your cat swallowed a long string and needs stomach surgery. While pet insurance may only cover 10 to 50 percent (the websites say up to 90 percent) of the costs, it may pay off if your cat is accident-prone. It also may be cheaper for you to keep him indoors, as he'd be less likely to be bitten by a dog, attacked by another cat, or sustain trauma from "outdoor living." Regardless of how much you cat-proof your house, veterinary medicine can be expensive as the quality of care improves, so pet insurance may be a smart option.

Can I dye my cat's hair?

Personally, I believe cats are beautiful au naturel. While some people and veterinarians may have ethical problems with dyeing cat hair, it is generally safe as long as you use an animal-friendly, veterinary dermatologist–recommended product. Cat hair isn't the same as human hair, however, so pick the hair product carefully, as cats are *very* sensitive to drugs; their livers weren't designed to break down toxins, drugs, and chemicals as well as other species. I have seen a few dog patients with dyed hair, particularly around Halloween time, and while I hate to admit it, it's really cute on some patients (poodles, anyone?). That said, dyed cats are more of a rarity, except for those rare pictures circulating on the Internet (which sparks ethical debate on whether or not we should be dyeing cats!). What is it about a cat painted with a clown face that causes grins and squeals in kids (and adults) across the nation but frowns all around from all those painted cats? The feline species probably doesn't appreciate hair dyeing any more than it relishes a kitty costume. However, if you're adamant about doing it, I advocate using a vegetable-based, animal-friendly, environmentally friendly, safe dye. If your cat has sensitive skin, skin allergies, or abnormal liver problems, don't attempt this without seeking the advice of your veterinarian—or safer yet, take out your creativity on yourself: dye your *own* hair, not your cat's.

Can I paint my cat's nails?

Don't even think about it. No self-respecting cat would *ever* sit still long enough for you to paint his or her nails. If you really want Princess to have glamorous paws, Soft Paws (as discussed in "Is declawing cats cruel?" in chapter 2) are a noninvasive way to give your cat a "pedicure," and they come in every color variety you desire. For you color-obsessed cat owners, you can try holiday colors, mix-and-match colors (a different color for each foot or nail), clear (for you au naturel types), white, black, every rainbow color, or even multicolor combos like pink with gray tips.

Is there kitty day care? Should I set up playdates for my cat?

Ever hear the 5 A.M. screams from cats fighting outside? Cats are like women—they don't like each other on first in-troduction and are instantly suspicious and leery. Cats are independent and aloof and don't crave the attention of other four-legged animals, which is why you never see any kitty day care facilities out there. With the exception of lions, cheetahs, and female domestic cats (who live with their offspring), cats are as asocial as animals come.[2] While some cats may get along with a housemate after adequate adjustment time, they generally get stressed meeting random cats. You'll notice hissing, fur fluffing, spraying, growling, and sudden fur-a-flying. Unlike your happy golden retriever who loves to play with everyone, kitty day care isn't a hit for a reason. While cats are curious and may like to watch the world go by through a glass window, they don't want to play or wrestle with a random strange cat. Unless your cats are well adapted to, say, your neighbor's cat or your family member's cat, they generally prefer not to have playdates. Keeps their turf cleaner with less bloodshed.

Can I take my cat on road trips with me?

Maybe I'm just the unfortunate owner of two cats that despise cars and traveling, but I have to use "better living through chemicals" (i.e., I have to use illicit veterinary drugs to take the edge off) just to get my cats into the car. Within the first few minutes, Seamus and Echo start panting, drooling, screaming, howling, running around, throwing themselves at windows, and massively shedding. Thanks to drugs, they tolerate car rides much better, but it's still stressful for all three of us. Because I prefer for them not to live half their lives in a zombie-induced, drugged state, I rarely travel with them unless I'm moving or there's a veterinary emergency.

I recently had a client who traveled all over the country to horse shows with her cat. Apparently, her cat was so used to it that he actually looked forward to the road trips. He'd sit on the dashboard, staring at trucks and cars passing by. If your cat is like this, then it's fine to travel with him, as long as you take certain precautions. The biggest thing is to check with your state laws. It's likely illegal for your cat to be running around free in the car (Hey, do what I say, not what I do!), because if he gets stuck under the brake pedal, you'll either (a) have an accident or (b) have a very smooshed cat. My other word to the wise is to make sure you crate your cat *before* you open the door. You may think you have a good hold of your cat, but when a cat squirms, he's outta there, and can easily escape your grasp, putting himself in danger.

Can I bring my cat to a hotel?

If you're leaving for a weekend getaway, spare your cat the stress of travel and leave him at home. Cats don't like sudden changes in life, whether it be changes in diet, environment, or anything related to their comforts of home (like where their kitty litter boxes live or what type of kitty litter they are used to having). Unless you're traveling for a longer duration (like driving cross-country) or happen to have that rare cat that is well adapted and loves to ride shotgun in the car, try to minimize Kitty's car time—she'll appreciate it. When road-tripping, map out your route carefully so you know what cat-friendly hotels are along the way. On the Internet, you can easily find pet-friendly hotels that will allow your cat a place to rest with you. Most hotels will take cats and small dogs, but make sure your pet is welcome before pushing your luck (as the constant meowing at the door may be a dead give-away). When taking your cat to your plush hotel, make sure you bring a small litter box, a secure carrier, spare kitty litter in Ziploc bags, a small scooper, a collar and form of identification (that should be on your cat at all times), food, bowls, and a favorite toy and snack, just in case she has a hard time adapting and needs some familiar comforts from home. Most important, leave a note on the door and a message with the front desk that no one open the door, as the last thing you need is for the maid to assist your cat in escaping from Motel 6.

Can I take my cat on the plane?

Cats don't understand the loud noises, vibrations, feelings of nausea, and the general concept of air travel. If you are only flying for a weeklong trip, consider whether it's worth putting your cat through so much stress. He may prefer to be sleeping at home instead of spending the trip confused and fearful of loud noises. Here are a few tips about safe air travel that you should consider before flying with your cat in tow.

First, schedule an appointment with your veterinarian for a routine examination. This typically needs to be dated within ten days of travel, depending on the state, country of origin, and airline requirements. Your cat has to have a current health certificate to verify that he's healthy, isn't carrying any external or internal parasites (fleas, ticks, or gastrointestinal worms), and is current on his vaccines. Remember to carry his health certificate with you at all times while traveling, as it may need to be shown to airport personnel, police officers, and border control. I also photocopy the health certificate and tape it to an envelope on the carrier as an extra precaution. (Of course, I'm pretty anal retentive and neurotic about my pets, but hey, you're still reading my book, so you may think I'm OK.) While you are at your veterinarian getting your health certificate, ask the staff to trim your cat's nails at the same time, so they don't hook in the bedding, appall the staff, or scratch you during a stressful freak-out. Ask your veterinarian about a sedative like oral acepromazine or Torbugesic, but not Valium (see "Can I give my cat my Valium?" in chapter 4). It's worth having some sedative just in case your cat freaks out—and no, you can't take it.

If you do need to fly with your cat, make sure to thoroughly investigate travel plans with your airline company. Different airline companies have crate size restrictions, specific crate types or brands, temperature restrictions, identification or labeling protocols, and water and food requirements. Check with the airline weeks in advance to make sure you aren't scrambling to order a specific carrier at the last minute. Ideally, see if you can take your cat on board in a soft-sided carrier (like a Sherpa carrier). This often requires an additional animal fee of $50 to $100, but it's worth it. If you do this, your cat is supposed to stay in the carrier under the seat *at all times* (which may require some sedation); this is to help respect those stuffy, uptight people around you who do not like cats or are allergic. After all, we have to respect their airplane space too.

When flying your cat in cargo (i.e., the scary bottom of the plane), book a direct flight so your cat doesn't have to endure a long layover. If you are flying during the summer, make sure to pick flights that are early morning or late evening to avoid peak heat hours. During the winter, pick the shortest flight possible and provide a secure but snug blanket to help keep your cat warm. If you are going to carry your cat on board, book a non-peak but direct flight, as that may be less stressful for you both.

Next, purchase (or borrow) the appropriate-sized crate and slowly acclimate your cat to it—in other words, don't plunk him in it for the first time on the night before you travel. Leave it open and around the house for weeks before you fly, so your cat can investigate it so he won't be as scared when the time approaches. You might even consider purchasing a calming pheromone spray called Feliway (see "What's Feliway and what does one do with these feline pheromones?" in chapter 5). If you spray a small hand towel or T-shirt and leave it in the carrier on the day of the flight, it may actually help relax him. Try this at home first, to make sure he likes pheromones. ("Ugh. Not Drakkar again!") Also, unless your cat is a diabetic or has underlying metabolic problems where he can't go without food, don't feed him for ten to twelve hours prior to air travel; this is to prevent him from vomiting from the stress and nausea. Have fun sitting with that under your seat!

Before you even leave for the airport, make sure to provide lots of extra time to find the animal drop-off area (if your cat is going into the cargo space) or to get through security, as it often takes longer with all the paperwork if you're carrying your cat on board. And lastly, because we all hear about those horror stories of cats getting lost for weeks in the cargo hold (only to survive and end up in Idaho), make sure your carrier or crate is very well secured!

Does Tigger like to wear costumes or clothes?

Cats don't want to be donned in clothing, which restricts their ability to escape, run, and be agile. That said, some cats are surprisingly tolerant of their owners' idiosyncrasies and don't fight having a Superman cape and hat on. If you notice your cat rolling, scratching, or acting paralyzed in fear, do him a favor and take the costume off (but not without getting a quick picture or video first). Otherwise, I'll be forced to call PETA.

How do I prevent kitty dreadlocks?

While grooming and brushing your cat may not seem like a fun Friday night activity, you should be doing it as a good pet owner, especially if you have a long-haired cat. Fat cats have a tendency to develop butt mats, as they're too fat to turn around or contort themselves elegantly to groom. So be a good cat owner: brush your cat (and help him lose some weight too!). If you can't find the time, pay a groomer to do it for you. Otherwise, not only will you have lots of hair ball poop or vomit bombs to avoid on the floor, but your cat will develop painful, ugly mats in the fur. These can only be removed by shaving them off and can cause redness and inflammation to the skin under the big mat. Let your groomer or your veterinarian shave them off, as I've seen far too many grooming "accidents"; it's far cheaper to pay a groomer several times than it is to visit the kitty ER even once!

Can my cat give me fleas if he sleeps with me?

If your cat goes outdoors, I recommend using a veterinary-prescribed, feline flea preventative (such as Advantage), as it's easier to *prevent* flea infestation than chemically bomb your house later. One little flea produces thousands of eggs, and you want to nip it in the bud before your whole family's itching. While fleas will typically stay on your cat, they can jump off onto you or your furniture. So, yes, you can get fleas from your cat if he or she is infested with parasites. While it's unlikely your cat is going to transmit the plague to you, his fleas could. Not worth chancing!

Using a veterinary-prescribed topical ointment (which is typically applied between the shoulder blades on the skin so Kitty can't lick it off) is the most effective way to prevent fleas. Pet store or grocery store flea collars only work well around the neck area, so please, save your money. When using flea preventative, it's also important to realize that cats are very sensitive to drugs and certain medications owing to a decreased liver glutathione metabolism (in other words, their liver can't filter drugs well). Hence, cat-specific flea prevention can be used *only* on cats. Do not use dog flea prevention, as this may cause severe or even fatal reactions (such as seizing, drooling, salivating, or muscle tremors). Big cat does not equal small dog! While this seems intuitive, I see flea product toxicity quite frequently in my practice, as people can't seem to read the label DO NOT USE ON CATS. When in doubt, consult your veterinarian for flea control (and see "Are all flea products the same?" in chapter 8).

In general, a veterinary-recommended flea preventative is most effective. Since cats are such neurotic groomers (and can usually chew and groom off a tick), and because they don't usually go hiking in the woods, it's rare for your cat to get tick-infested (unless you live in Old Lyme, Connecticut, and your cat lives outdoor 100 percent of the time!). If the latter is the case, you may need a flea *and* tick preventative (like Frontline). I usually believe in using the least amount of chemicals necessary to treat something, so that extra tick preventative isn't necessary in most cats—it's mostly for those minute, tiny, dirty tapeworm- and plague-carrying fleas!

Can I give my cat a breath mint?

No self-respecting cat would ever eat a breath mint. Your cat would just expect you to deal with her breath. Unfortunately, the closest you'll ever get to giving your cat a mint is to give her some fresh catnip, which is a relative of the mint family. While it won't make her breath any better, she'll be so loopy and happy that she won't care about her bad breath! Still, your cat likely won't eat fresh (non-catnip-variety) mint just to freshen her breath, so if you're that concerned, you should brush her teeth.

In dogs, we worry about the toxicity of xylitol, which is an artificial sweetener in certain types of gum and breath mints. Unfortunately, it can result in life-threatening low blood sugar or, in severe cases, even liver failure. When in doubt, don't give your dog a breath mint. Luckily, we don't usually see this toxicity in cats, as they don't typically rummage through your purse in search of gum.

Which cultures still worship cats?

It is well known that Egyptians initially worshipped cats owing to their usefulness in killing poisonous snakes and vermin, thereby protecting their granaries and crops. Archaeologists have found hieroglyphics, temples, necropolises, and graves with mummified cats, helping prove to dog lovers just how great this species has been and continues to be. Evidence of domestication of cats was found as early as 6000–5000 BC based on archaeological findings on the island of Cyprus,[3] while European domesticated cats may have originated from Egypt between 3000–2000 BC.[4] Egyptians had catlike goddesses such as the Sekhmet (who had the head of a lion), a goddess of war and sun, and Mafdet, a goddess of protection. The citizens of the city of Bubastis also worshipped cats based on the goddess Bast (who was the goddess of protection, the sun, and the moon). Egyptians worshipped their cats so much that they chose to be buried with them and often shaved their eyebrows as a sign of mourning when their cat died.

Through the centuries, though, cats have also been on the other side of the coin. Instead of being worshipped, sometimes they were condemned as "of the devil." Pope Gregory IX denounced black cats as satanic and thousands of cats were burned alive in 1233. While the worship of cats has died down (they are now sadly viewed as pests in many countries, owing to pet overpopulation), the domestication of cats has spread throughout the world.

Currently, the Japanese culture has a modern-day catlike goddess: a famous cat figurine called the Maneki Neko, which is often referred to as the "Beckoning Cat" based on its one upright raised forelimb and paw. Traditionally, the raised right paw was supposed to beckon wealth and luck, while the left paw brought customers. For this reason, you may find it at the entrance of shops, bars, and restaurants throughout Japan. In fact, one of the Pokémon characters resembles this cat figurine. Not sure if Hello Kitty originated from this famous cat, but hey, it's nice to see cats still idolized.

Do I have to teach my cat to use the litter box?

Cats make great apartment pets because they learn to pee and poop in a litter box. Most important, they are smart enough to have some poor sucker clean it out (i.e., you and me). When I first adopted Seamus as a kitten, I placed him in the litter box and scratched his paws in the litter so he realized where the box was and what he was supposed to do. Within the first use, he figured it out and I've never had problems since. Thankfully, most cats instinctively know how to use a litter box and require little training, so, no, you usually don't have to teach your cat how to do it.

Can I train my cat to use the toilet?

Thanks to Mr. Jinx, the Byrnes' cat from *Meet the Parents*, toilet training your cat has become popular. The rare cat is toilet trained but, with persistence and patience, can indeed be trained. Of course, just like your husband, it'll be very difficult to teach him to flush, but we'll take what we can get, right?

Now that you've decided to toilet train your cat, begin by checking out all your available resources, as there are multiple different ways of attempting this.[5] There are great articles on the Internet, along with books and videos dedicated just to toilet training your cat. The biggest thing you'll learn when you read through the wealth of information out there is that toilet training a cat takes lots and lots of patience. As you know, cats don't really handle change very well, and when in doubt, it's always important to take it slow while adjusting your cat to your toilet (or to revert back a few steps if you think you're pushing Tigger too quickly). First, toilet training your cat works best if you happen to have more than one bathroom. Use one designated toilet just for Tigger, making sure to duct tape the toilet lid *up,* and the toilet seat *down.* Next, move your uncovered kitty litter box into the bathroom, and place it right next to the toilet. Make sure Tigger knows where you moved it, so you don't have any accidental messes in the house. Over the course of several days, gradually increase the height of the litter box, by securely placing newspapers or even telephone books under the box. Word of advice: don't use slippery or glossy magazines, because making the litter box slide while Tigger's inside will send him running, potentially shattering all hopes of toilet training! Your goal is to gradually get the bottom of the litter box to the level of the toilet seat. Once Tigger gets used to peeing on top of the world, secure your kitty litter box on top of the toilet, gradually decreasing the amount of litter in the box. Once he's used to being king of the toilet and up that high, replace the litter box with a well-secured metal roasting pan that should sit between the toilet seat and the rim. Fill it with kitty litter, and gradually make sure Tigger adjusts to this new contraption. Gradually decrease the amount of kitty litter in the pan (making sure to keep the pan as clean as possible). Then, cut a small hole in the metal pan, allowing the urine to drain into the toilet. Over the next few days to weeks, cut a larger and larger hole in the pan. This will gradually increase the diameter of the hole, allowing Tigger an adjustment period while he learns where to place his feet on the periphery of the hole or toilet seat. Make sure to use flushable kitty litter, as it will fall into the toilet as your cat scrapes and cleans. With steady consistency and reward, hopefully you can transition your cat from the pan to the toilet! Now if we could only teach him how to flush . . .

There are some people who are against toilet training cats because they worry about cat feces filling our water supply (see "Clay, clumping, or crystals?" in this chapter and "Do I have to get rid of my cat when I'm pregnant?" in chapter 9). That said, the environmental impact of not having to use hundreds to thousands of pounds of kitty litter (which sit in the landfill) over your cat's life span may still make Al Gore smile. Either way, you have to pick your environmental battle.

How many kitty litter boxes do I need?

The nice thing about a litter box is that you can hide it in the basement or corner of your laundry room. For you poor apartment or studio dwellers, you'll have to get more creative when it comes to hiding litter boxes in your small abode. Personally, I can't stand the smell of kitty litter (or the presents left inside), so I don't like having it in my kitchen or bedroom. Since bathrooms are generally odiferous to begin with, hiding a kitty litter box in the corner of the bathroom somewhere is probably best for you non-basement people.

The general recommendation is to have $n + 1$ litter boxes. In other words, if you have three cats, you should have four litter boxes. While this seems excessive, remember that cats are affected by litter box husbandry and cleanliness, and you'd much rather have extra litter box cleaning duty than inappropriate urination in the house. Cats are very territorial and prefer not to share. You may find that each cat picks their own particular litter box. Since variety is the spice of life, why not be able to choose from multiple toilets?

Should I buy a covered or uncovered litter box?

The next time you're in a pet store, take a look around—you'll be amazed at the variety of litter box choices that are available. You can purchase tall boxes, short boxes, small boxes, huge boxes, boxes with automatic scoopers, boxes of different shapes and colors, and covered and uncovered boxes. Most come with a lid, but not everyone chooses to use them. When in doubt, splurge a little—after all, litter boxes pretty much last a lifetime. Personally, I tolerate only covered litter boxes in my household. I like them because they help keep the kitty litter dust and smell in, prevent excessive kicking of litter onto the floor, and are more aesthetically friendly to houseguests.

In a multicat household, the more submissive cat may feel "trapped" in a covered litter box by an approaching cat and may be too timid to enter a covered litter box if she's feeling ganged up on. This may then result in inappropriate urination (i.e., peeing in your laundry basket, your plants, the basement, or on your down comforter). If your cats get along fine, try covered litter boxes, as it dramatically decreases the "dirtiness" of having a litter box around in your house. You may even notice that your friends come around to visit you more. If you're not sure, leave a few options out there for your cats: a few covered and uncovered litter boxes, a few different locations, and different types of litter to see what your cats prefer.

How often do I *really* need to clean my cat's litter box?

While it seems trivial, an unclean litter box can result in serious behavioral and medical problems in cats. For that reason, we neurotic types clean litter boxes daily. If that's too much for you, litter boxes should be scooped out *at least* every other day. Of course, this depends on how many cats you have (just because you added $n + 1$ litter boxes doesn't mean you can clean less frequently!). The more cats you have, the more frequently the boxes should be scooped out. While it's a dirty job, it *really* should be done for the best interest of your cats.

If you notice your cat scratching *outside* the litter box instead of inside (What's a cat gotta do to get you to clean the litter box? Helllllo!), it's his way of telling you that the litter box is disgusting and he doesn't want to get his feet filthy while he's attempting to cover up his poop inside. If you just cleaned the litter box and he's still doing it, it's likely from a bad memory of getting his feet urine-soaked or dirty while in the box, so unless you want a pet that poops in random places, get in there and scoop!

Some cats will "hold it" and urinate as infrequently as possible to avoid stepping into a dirty, filthy, full litter box. Instead of urinating two to three times a day, Tigger will tighten up and only go once a day. This makes his urine get more concentrated and could make crystals and urine debris plug up the tip of his penis and cause him to get a life-threatening feline urethral obstruction (FUO). With FUO, cats may have stones, crystals, or mucous plugs in their urethra that prevent them from being able to urinate. Not only is this painful, but it can also lead to temporary kidney failure, electrolyte abnormalities, vomiting, lethargy, arrhythmias, and death. So to help prevent problems like this or even diseases like feline lower urinary tract disease or sterile cystitis, scoop! (see "Why do cats lick down there?" and "What is FLUTD and how do I treat it?" in chapter 2).

The other added benefit of scooping frequently is that it helps you detect medical problems earlier. If Tigger isn't urinating, you'll notice when there's no urine in the litter box for two days. If Tigger becomes a diabetic, he may be making larger and larger clumps and your whole litter box will be one huge clump after its weekly cleaning. But you'll never be able to tell this if you're not scooping enough. If Tigger is acting constipated or having diarrhea, you won't find out until days later, and by then it'll be a bigger (and more expensive) medical treatment! As tedious as it is, please do your wife a favor and flush, and your cat a favor and scoop.

Clay, clumping, or crystals?

We're bombarded by pet store advertising when it comes to what type of litter to use. Basically, it's all about personal preference. While living with my vet school housemate, I asked her why she used clay ("Hellooo! Old school!"). She said that's what she had always used (my roomie was from the 1960s generation, when clay was hip). After being fed up with the smell and mess, I decided to change her litter to clumping one day. She was wowed, dumbfounded, an instant convert, and she hasn't gone back since. Crystal, her cat, loved it too.

Clay litter was first introduced in 1947 by Edward Lowe, who used to sell clay to garage owners to soak up oil and gasoline spills.[6] When he realized it worked well in kitty litter boxes, it became an instant success. Since then, kitty litter has become a multimillion-dollar business. Why didn't I think of this first? Clay is still a great absorber and cheap as dirt (well, clay), but it's more environmentally unfriendly as you have to dump out the whole litter box once it's full (in other words, once a week). Like its name suggests, clay doesn't clump, so you can't just scoop out nice, neat clumps of urine to clean the box. Notice how those large forty-pound bags of clay litter are cheaper than the twenty-five-pound bucket of clumping litter? You get what you pay for.

Since the early 1980s, cat lover (and, oh yeah, biochemist) Thomas Nelson discovered that a particular type of clay, bentonite, formed clumps in the presence of moisture, thanks to its "stacks of SiO_4 sandwiched between two sheets of octahedrally coordinated aluminum, magnesium, or iron"[7] and voilà . . . clumping kitty litter. Because bentonite can absorb up to ten times its own weight, it is able to bind and hold water (or urine) firmly in place, resulting in that tight clump. Bentonite is dug up from the ground and processed into either granules or a powder form, and apparently we cat lovers are using a lot of it. According to a U.S. Geological Survey, approximately 987,000 metric tons of this clumping clay was mined in 2003 for cat litter.[8] Popular stuff, right?

This clumping litter is much better than the clay stuff, in my opinion. First of all, it's more pet-owner friendly—it requires less cleaning and work than clay litter. Second, clumping litter is more environmentally friendly than the clay stuff. With clumping litter, you don't have to completely dump out the whole litter box of clumping litter (ever)—just lift out the nice, scoopable urine and fecal ball clumps, and voilà, all done. I only harp on this because when owners bring in their cat to the ER for urinary problems, I quiz them on their kitty litter habits. That's when I learn that most cat owners don't really know about kitty litter husbandry—in other words, how to take care of their kitty litter box in the easiest, most efficient, most environmentally friendly, least dirty way. Some clients tell me they dump out the whole litter box (and all that clumping litter) every week. Yikes—no need, folks! You and your cat's carbon footprints are contributing to the overfilled landfills and making Al Gore very angry. Not only is this expensive, but it's really wasteful. If you really want to know, I only *completely empty* and bleach out the litter box a few times a year or so. OK, maybe once or twice a year. Seriously. While we animal lovers would love to blame human babies and their disposable, environmentally unfriendly diaper waste, I'm afraid we can't—it turns out that kitty litter takes up a massive amount of our landfills. Remarkably, the Bureau of Waste Management estimates that approximately 8 billion pounds of kitty litter fills landfills each year.[9] My other environmental trick of the trade is to leave a covered, empty kitty litter bucket lined with a plastic bag right next to the kitty litter box. It's a perfect container to scoop and store stuff in until it's full of clumps and crap. It makes it oh so easy to scoop, contains the smell in the empty bucket, and saves a few plastic bags while making it more convenient to clean.

Even if clumping litter marketers say you can flush litter down the toilet, I'm not an advocate of this practice, as I don't feel that it's safe to have our water supply contaminated with cat feces. There's a lot of controversy on this topic, especially when it comes to people toilet training their cats (see

"Can I train my cat to use the toilet?" in this chapter). That said, many sea otter deaths reported in the northwestern United States have recently been linked to toxoplasmosis, a bacterial infection shed in cat feces. While there's no definitive, scientific proof that cats caused this, save the world and all the other fuzzy creatures and please don't flush.

Finally, the $20 bottle of crystals. Is it worth it? Being that you likely have to buy it monthly (depending on how many cats you have), it's the most expensive option when it comes to kitty litter. That said, some people love crystals because they absorb odor very well and allow you to scoop out the feces. Keep in mind that crystals will never clump, so you can't expect to remove large piles of urine. Rather, the crystals work by absorption. Once the crystals have turned yellow, they will no longer absorb and the whole litter box has to be dumped and cleaned (approximately every one to two weeks, depending on how many cats use the litter box). Also, having accidentally stepped on these crystals before . . . ouch! I can't imagine that it is fun to urinate on dull shards of silica gel; it reminds me of walking on a nice sandy beach (clumping) versus a pebbled beach . . . and I prefer the former.

Other options include using silica gel pearls, recycled newspaper, pine or cedar sawdust, corncob litter, or even wheat husks. It's all personal preference, and priority should go to what your cat wants, not what you want. Just keep in mind that these other options are expensive, slightly less effective (they don't form a tight clump, making it harder to scoop and clean), but are more environmentally friendly. That said, I'd rather not have my cats pee all over my house owing to behavior problems just to save the earth. (Trust me, I make a difference in other ways—I promise!) Also, animal behaviorists find that cats prefer *clumping* litter to any other type, so I'd trust them. If you're thinking of switching and experimenting with new litters, remember that cats do not do well with acute change. They are creatures of habit and want gradual changes; otherwise, they may inappropriately urinate around the house just to spite you.

How big of a clump is normal?

My sister should know that she gets lifelong access to free veterinary questions, right? (Oh, if only you were so lucky!) Which is why I was so shocked when I went out to visit her recently. Being that she's pregnant, her husband now cleans the litter box (and he hates cats, poor guy). Being the nice veterinary sister that I am, I decided to clean the litter box for them while I was visiting (typical veterinary response: I smell cat pee, therefore I must scoop) only to be appalled by the size of Elliot's clumps! I rushed to my sister and quizzed her further: Is Elliot drinking more, 'cause he's sure peeing a lot! She and my brother-in-law had no idea, so I clued them in that if their cat's clump is bigger than its head, it was probably inappropriate. That's when I also pointed out that Elliot shouldn't be sitting by the water bowl for more than few minutes at a time ("Well, I guess I have been filling it more . . .").

So, just how big should the clump be? It depends on multiple factors: whether your cat is the type to hold it all day, how many urine clumps or trips to the litter box he likes to make (in other words, one huge clump versus three smaller piles), what type of food you feed him (canned food may make him pee a little bit more), and how often you clean out the litter box. In general, if you slowly notice the clumps getting bigger and bigger, bring your cat to a vet. If the piles are bigger than your clenched fist (OK, *my* clenched fist, in case you're a big, burly guy), then they're too big, and you should bring your cat to a vet to check his kidneys, thyroid, and blood sugar.

How can I make the litter box smell less unpleasant?

As much as I'd love to give you an easy answer, there's simply no way to make the litter box smell like roses. In general, the more frequently you scoop, the less ammonia smell will accumulate. After only having one cat, I was shocked by how much dirtier and more expensive it was to add one additional cat into my home. Granted, it's well worth the companionship, but still.

Try a covered litter box to help trap those nasty smells in—while the smell doesn't go away, it doesn't dissipate all over your house (after all, they can't light matches, right?). Also, while I'm not sure those little charcoal filters on the top of the litter box cover help, they certainly don't hurt. If you're scooping neurotically and it still stinks, dump out your litter, clean and bleach your litter box a few times a year, and start all over again. Finally, having a supersensitive snoot myself, I use the occasional animal-friendly Arm & Hammer deodorant powder in the litter boxes, and I have a large array of air fresheners in the basement. Gotta hide that cat smell from the boyfriend or he'll never let me get more cats . . .

Why does my cat suck on my cashmere sweater?

If you just paid a lot for that new cashmere or wool sweater, hide it from your cat. Some cats develop "wool sucking," which may be apparent when your sweaters, quilts, and blankets have cute little holes all over them. Wool sucking is more commonly seen in the Oriental breeds, such as Siamese cats, and while there's been no official link to say that it is hereditary, you probably shouldn't breed your new cat just in case, as this habit is highly annoying and expensive. While this habit seems like a minor problem, it can be quite destructive over time. Some people think that wool sucking is an obsessive and misguided attempt at nursing. It may be the lanolin smell in the wool that reminds your cat of the scent of his mother's nipples, or even the taste of animal hair in his mouth that is soothing to him. While it's not dangerous to your cat (unless he swallows lots of wool and it gets stuck in his stomach or intestines), it can be quite damaging to your wardrobe and frustrating to your clothing budget.

The best way to prevent wool sucking is to put any tempting material out of your cat's reach. Apparently, Mom was right when she told you to clean your room. Don't tempt your cat (or your sweater's fate) by leaving things all over the place. If that doesn't work, you can go to the Salvation Army and pick up a cheap, already-holey sweater, drown it in Cajun pepper or Bitter Apple, and see if your cat learns that it's not so nice after all. Another option is to increase the fiber content in your cat's diet or to supplement fiber as a treat; it's cheap and easy enough to run to your local pet store and purchase some cat grass (it's like having a Chia Pet in your house). Unfortunately, the fiber trick doesn't work for all cats. Also, try increasing your cat's exercise or minimizing his stress instead (see "How do I exercise my fat, indoor cat?" in chapter 5), so he's too tuckered out at the end of the night to suck on wool. If all else fails, you can contact your veterinarian for feline floaters (drugs) to help minimize the wool sucking.

Do cats get high from catnip, and can I use it?

Catnip, otherwise known as *Nepeta cataria,* is a common North American plant that can be easily grown in a pot. Catnip acts as a stimulant in cats, although 10 to 50 percent of cats seem to be unaffected by it, which may be due to genetics. The effects of catnip are due to *nepetalactone,* and it results in a short-lived, nonaddictive euphoric feel. You may notice cats rubbing themselves on the catnip, being more active or affectionate, purring, or rolling in the catnip. Because many cats enjoy catnip, you can apply some to a scratching post or new cat bed to increase the likelihood that they'll use it. Yes, this is the cat equivalent of getting high. And no, you can't use it (it won't work).

What's kitty crack?

Kitty crack is the street name for ketamine, a drug we use to sedate and castrate cats. Sometimes we use it on dogs, but it's more commonly used on cats, as "doggy crack" doesn't have the same hip ring to it. This is an NMDA-receptor antagonist, which is a fancy way of saying that it is a dissociative drug that separates the pain from the pain receptor. This drug is extremely dangerous for humans and is illegal for nonveterinary use. Believe it or not, I have had clients ask me for it directly and police officers calling for the "street price." ("Officer, I have no idea what the street price is, but I can tell you that based on your weight to be neutered, it would be about $300.") Please be a good pet owner and don't hit up your vet at the next party.

Chapter 4
KRAZY KITTY

PEOPLE are constantly asking me if I think cats have an "inner sense." I didn't think so until I met Crystal. My vet school housemate's cat Crystal was never affectionate toward me (despite my saving her from another decade of crappy clay litter and converting her mom to clumping— see "Clay, clumping, or crystals?" in chapter 3). In fact, even though I lived with her for several months, she never allowed me to pick her up. Apparently, Crystal was really, really shy, and I was likely too hyper for her, as she ran away at the sound of my scurrying, quick-paced feet. Once, after a traumatic, exhausting day in veterinary school, I came home emotionally wasted and raw. One of my favorite Hanoverian horses from the farm that I worked on at Cornell had died in my arms while we lay in the straw. Her owner wouldn't euthanize her despite our protests, and she was slowly dying from septic shock and in severe pain. It broke my heart to see her slip away, and she died with her head in my lap, with my tears dripping down on her as she finally departed. By the time I got home, I stumbled upstairs, sat on my sofa, and wept. Crystal, who never, ever approached me, came and sat on my chest, purring away for the next half hour. She *knew* . . .

Cats seem to have an intriguing ability to read our minds, don't they? Want to know what your cat's *really* thinking? Want to find out if cats really have emotions, or if we are anthropomorphizing their feelings? When Max poops on your expensive down comforter while you are away, is he doing it intentionally out of vengeance? Not sure if your cat cries, mourns, or gets jealous? Maybe your cat is crazy and needs a pet psychic, behaviorist, or shrink. Find out if you can give your Valium to your cat (the short answer is no!). Better yet, how do you explain your cat's crazy habits like singling out the only cat hater in the crowd, only to rub fur and dander all over him? To find out about all of your cat's (mostly lovable) idiosyncrasies, read on!

Are there cat whisperers or pet shrinks out there?

The people who can fix our freaky felines are from the American College of Veterinary Behaviorists (ACVB). These are veterinarians who have completed veterinary school and an additional two- to three-year residency program in animal behavior. While ACVB board-certified behaviorists probably don't appreciate being called pet shrinks, they do work to ensure that appropriate training, behavioral modification, and desensitization training occur to help your crazy kitty. This is an important field, because most shelters find that animals are surrendered or even euthanized because of poor human-animal bonds that stem from the animals' inappropriate or undesirable behavior. After all, it's a whole lot harder to bond with your cat if he's peeing in the house or when he attacks your ankles and draws blood, right?

Common cat complaints that justify a visit to the behaviorist include intercat aggression, urine marking, inappropriate elimination, scratching, aggression toward people, and nocturnal restlessness.[1] In other words, your nocturnal cat is driving you nuts and you need some help to stay sane! If necessary, pet Prozac can be dispensed by your veterinary behaviorist.

There are also cat whisperers out there; these are breeders, shelter socializers, or just people with extensive animal experience who offer their services on a freelance basis. They often use techniques adapted from veterinary behaviorists, but each usually has his or her own methodology and spin on common behavioral modification techniques. It's important to consult your veterinarian or do extensive, well-rounded research prior to making a decision on how best to treat your cat, as these guys can't dispense pet Prozac.

Can I give my cat my Valium?

Don't even *think* about giving your cat your Valium. Rare liver failure (otherwise known as acute hepatic necrosis) can be seen with repeated *oral* doses of Valium,[2] and while it's periodically dispensed for behavioral problems or for sedation, it isn't worth the risk to your cat. While this drug reaction is relatively rare, it carries a 95 percent death rate in those affected by oral Valium. So no, it's not OK to give your cat your meds. Rest assured in knowing that the intravenous form of Valium that we veterinarians commonly use is very safe and not associated with liver failure.

Are cats vengeful?

Animal behaviorists say that we project a lot of our feelings onto animals and that dogs and cats don't experience the same emotions of anger, jealousy, or vengefulness the way that humans do. Being a cat owner, however, I can attest that cats are vengeful. Ever notice how your cats ignore you when you come back from a business trip? Notice how you come home to a destroyed house? All your countertop items now on the floor? I can almost picture my cats purposely knocking cereal boxes onto the floor just to spite me (what I'd like to know is how their two nonopposable thumbs can open the plastic so all the cereal spills). Granted, maybe they just had a sudden, unusually playful urge, but I still think it's out of revenge. After all, they never do it when I'm home or when I've had a long day at work. Apparently, this is my cat punishment for leaving them for a few days without their permission.

Remember that we may be misinterpreting our cats' "vengefulness" from their feelings of stress. If you think your cat is purposely peeing on your down duvet while you're away, think again. High stress levels can result in a possible change in the pH of urine, predisposing cats to a sterile cystitis. So before you blame your cat, kindly recall that he may just not deal with stress well, and his way of showing it may be peeing outside the box. Echo and Seamus never poop outside of the box—unless I'm away. Whether it's from vengefulness or stress, I'll take dried poop over urine any day . . .

Do cats think?

That depends. Cats are really smart at, well, being cats. They can't do higher math, but they're pretty smart at ruling the roost, getting fat and lazy, and having every two-legged creature bow to their every command. Cats are smart enough to have someone else clean up their poop and are smart enough to beg for food at 5 A.M. But do they *think*?

Having had to dissect cat brains during freshman anatomy, I've seen how small their brains are, and it's nothing to write home about. Pound per pound, however, they have a bigger brain than a horse (that's not saying much, by the way). Yes, cats do think, but it's not to the same level that we humans do. Cats retain memory, know basic verbal cues (responding to their names), make sound associations (opening a can of food), and have basic survival knowledge (if I wake him up at 5 A.M., he'll feed me).

In the ER, I often see cats with severe traumatic brain injury from jumping out windows, being hit by cars, having their head stuck in a dog's mouth, or being accidentally stepped on (which is what happened to Seamus). It's quite amazing how neurologically impaired or comatose cats can be when they first enter the ER and how dramatically they improve a few days later. This goes to show you that either (a) they have the fastest nerve regeneration (which isn't true; otherwise we'd be able to cure paralyzed people), or (b) they don't have higher cognitive function to the levels that humans do (in other words, they don't have to use their brain to read and write). Thankfully, they are lovable regardless. It's like loving that big, dumb jock—so cute.

Do cats cry?

Cats do have some basic human emotions, but they don't cry from a higher-brain emotional response. While you may notice a small amount of clear fluid running from the corner of your cat's eyes, this is designed to naturally lubricate your cat's corneas. If it's excessive, it may be due to something irritating the eye, a corneal ulcer (a scratch on the clear surface of the eye), allergies, an upper respiratory infection (such as herpesvirus or calicivirus), a bacterial infection (chlamydia), or even a blocked nasolacrimal duct (which is the tube between your nose and eyes, and explains why your nose runs when you cry). If you notice that your kitty is weepy-eyed, it's probably not because you just adopted a dog. Rather, consider taking her to a veterinarian, as she likely has an upper respiratory infection or a scratch on her cornea causing her to tear excessively.

Do cats mourn?

In 1996 a study was performed by the American Society for the Prevention of Cruelty to Animals called the Companion Animal Mourning Project.[3] This study evaluated the response of surviving pets after losing a four-legged companion. Unfortunately, this study only looked at dogs, so we honestly can't truly generalize about cats from this study. Regardless, this study found that 63 percent of dogs either became quieter or vocalized more, while over 50 percent of pets become more affectionate to their caretaker. Thirty-six percent of dogs ate less than usual, while 11 percent become completely anorexic. This study found that 66 percent of dogs showed four or more behavioral changes secondary to the loss of a four-legged companion.[4]

I've had clients tell me that their remaining or surviving cat was constantly searching for their cat housemate, so I do believe that cats mourn. I have seen cats saddened by the absence of their two- or four-legged best friends. Thankfully, "time heals all things," and your cat may return back to his or her normal self after several weeks or months.

Why do cats rub their faces and bodies all over you, your furniture, and your houseguests?

While you may think it's cute that your cat is rubbing his face all over you, he's actually marking you as his. I find this to be cute at first but annoying, as Echo constantly head-butts my hand as I try to type this book. Of course, if you don't mind being the object of possession, then that's OK. When your cat is rubbing his face and chin all over you and your furniture, he's releasing scent glands (which are under his chin, around his eyes, and on his feet) that identify where he and you have been.

Why do cats seem to like the one houseguest who hates cats the most?

Ah, cats. They're like guys—once pursued, they're no longer interested. Cats play hard to get—they don't want to be petted by the person who wants to pet them; rather, they are peeved that this one person in the room is ignoring them. In order to wow them over to their dark cat side, they'll rub all over that allergic cat hater in an attempt to woo them over. Cats have an amazing inner sense and know exactly who to zoom in on. Nice black cashmere sweater? Hate cats? Allergic? I'll be right there . . .

What's my cat doing when he's kneading my blanket?

We in the veterinarian profession call this behavior "making muffins." Cats may knead a blanket, you, or their pet bed as a sign of comfort and relaxation. This behavior is more commonly seen in cats that have been separated from their mother as young kittens. This physical motion is an attempt to knead and get more milk out of their mother's breast, and cats often continue to do this as they enter adulthood. Some kittens who were hand-raised by humans may not demonstrate this, as they would have had a bottle placed in their mouth instead of having to do all the work of kneading for milk. Animal behaviorists also believe that cats "make muffins" as a marking technique, as they have scent glands in their pads. In general, don't worry—your cat isn't hungry or trying to get milk out of you. It's just an instinctive behavior for him. You should be flattered that your cat is so relaxed and happy to see you. After a long day at work, I capitalize on this by flipping on my back while in bed and letting Echo specifically "make muffins" (i.e., massage) my upper shoulders. One must earn their keep in a veterinary house, right?

Why does my cat attack me when I rub her belly?

Ever wonder why your cat acts like she wants you to pet her, only to scratch you when you do? When your cat rolls over to have you rub her beefy belly, be flattered or offended. She's either demonstrating (a) her vulnerability and submissiveness or (b) that she's queen of your palace and isn't worried that you have any predatorial dominance over her. Your cat is trusting that you won't viciously attack her underbelly, spilling all her intestines and disemboweling her in the process. Be excited—she trusts you! Of course, while she may feel comfortable in your presence, it doesn't mean she actually wants to be touched. Some cats enjoy the attention without the touches (like your last Friday night date) and will scratch you in return if you provide them with love when they just aren't ready for it.

Why does my cat attack my ankles?

Hate having your ankles run over by a grocery cart by that annoying person in back of you? Well, having your cat attack your ankles isn't much better. If your young or adolescent cat is doing this, he's attempting to stimulate you to play and may be pouncing on you in an attempt to chase or hunt you down. Remember that cats are huge predators, and the chase, catch, play, and kill are fun for them. Save your ankles and help redirect your cat's pent-up frustrations of play toward something inanimate so there's no bloodshed. The first step is to make sure that you're exercising your cat—a good ten- to fifteen-minute playtime each day will help wear him down (see "How do I exercise my fat, indoor cat?" in chapter 5). You can do this while you lazily read your newspaper by tossing him a pet mouse or a wad of paper, using a laser pointer, or using my cats' favorite toy—the squeaking feather on a string. Make sure to put some physical distance between you and the toy—you don't want your cat to associate the fun playtime with your ankle again.

Also, don't roughhouse with your cat with your hands or feet. If your cat is lying in a sunbeam, don't give him a belly rub with your foot just to pester him and wake him up, as he'll associate your limb with something annoying. Lastly, in desperate times, carry a water gun. If your cat is still attacking your ankles, give him a reminder squirt when he's attacking you. This negative reinforcement has to be given at the same time as the attack, or your cat won't associate the bad action of attacking your ankles with the water (for responsible, mature, water-gun-wielding adults only, please). Finally, while I don't recommend this unless you've tried *all* other options, having another housemate to tackle instead may be what he needs (another cat, not a human).

Do cats instinctively hate dogs?

Wildcats never had to worry about predators, as they were at the top of the food chain. As they got smaller and more domesticated, cats have now realized that they too have predators. Sucks not to be at the top, huh?

"Smaller" wildcats such as mountain lions, lynx, or bobcats realize that urban sprawl into their habitat is dangerous—for all parties involved—and that they are now prey to hunters and cars. Likewise, our domesticated cats have also instinctively learned to fear danger: the neighborhood bully, the local stray, cars, and other predators such as coyotes or the neighborhood mutt. When Simba sees a dog, he doesn't instinctively hate the dog; he just doesn't want to be its chew toy or next meal. His instinct is to run before he becomes intimately involved in the next circle of life.

In general, be careful acclimating dogs and cats together. Check with a veterinary behaviorist or consult your veterinarian if you're even thinking about introducing the two species together. Once cats and dogs have time to acclimate, they can potentially safely live together, depending on your breed of dog and how you've trained him. I adopted Seamus before I had any other pets, and he was used to being the top "dog" in the house; when I adopted my pit bull, JP, five months later (as a ten-pound puppy), Seamus instantly loved him. He groomed him, slept with him, and often jumped on him or tugged at his ear trying to get JP to wrestle with him. Of course, Seamus and JP were pretty much the same size when they met, so Seamus probably didn't view him as much competition. And the fact that Seamus had severe head trauma as a kitten just prior to meeting JP probably helped too (Seamus is a little slow and thinks it's OK to play-wrestle with a dog). Thankfully, they get along swimmingly.

How do I make my boyfriend like cats?

Now, this book is no *He's Just Not That into You,* so take my *dating* advice with a grain of salt. But what I've learned over the past three decades is that despite what you think (and hope), you cannot *change* men. But, as with a dog, you can potentially *train* them. That said, most men hate cats because they hate the unknown, right? Gentle exposure may be all that your boyfriend needs to slowly teach him to tolerate cats.

First, set the environment. Make sure your house doesn't smell like cat. When your boyfriend comes to visit and your litter boxes are filthy, the odiferous presence of ammonia is not going to win him over. Your cat will appreciate having a clean litter box too. Use air fresheners, candles, and scented plug-ins to help make your house more pleasant and airy for all. Initially (until he asks you to marry him), make the house look like cats don't live there (sorry, Kitty). You don't want him tripping over toys, bells, and cat vomit, right? Second, in order to make him love your cats, don't you *dare* ask him to do Kitty's chores. Absolutely do not ask him to scoop your cat's poop just because you're too cheap to hire a pet-sitter. You want to hide the fact that you have an animal crapping in your house for as long as you can. Third, use positive feedback. When your cat comes over to cuddle on the sofa with the two of you, interject with a quick "Want a beer?" or "Do you mind if I check to see what the baseball score is?" Reward positive behavior—in other words, make a positive association with your cat. Don't make it too obvious. If you take out a canine clicker training toy, he'll figure it out and bust your move. Lastly, try locking your cat out of the bedroom at night—Kitty's 3 A.M. nocturnal romping that you're used to may take a while for your boyfriend to love.

Does my cat have an inner clock, and how do I turn it off?

As all cat owners can attest, your cat is the most active just when you finally fall asleep. Some people actually believe that cats are doing their nocturnal jog around your head as they are "seeing ghosts." Unless you believe in your cat's sixth sense, there's likely no excuse for his crazy, nocturnal habits—just chalk it up to his catnip, the early morning hours, and his inner clock.

Unfortunately, their less-than-lovable nocturnal circadian rhythm may be due to two hormones: melatonin and vasopressin.[5] Melatonin is a neurohormone that controls the daily rhythms, helping with sleep and the reproductive cycle. While some people use this dietary supplement to help themselves sleep better, please don't use it on your cat to try to help him sleep through the night—thousands of years of being nocturnal can't be changed. Vasopressin, a hormone made in the hypothalamus, has mostly electrolyte and water-balance properties but recently has been implicated in crazy cat circadian rhythms. What it boils down to, however, isn't the fancy chemical name, but how you can prevent your cat from waking you up so early. Unfortunately, because cats are nocturnal by habit, there's not much you can do to change it. If you do figure it out, patent the idea, as you'll make millions from cat-loving morning people.

Here are a few ideas on how you can get some more sleep while still owning a cat. First, try exercising your cat before you go to bed. Solid exercise for ten to fifteen minutes should hopefully tire your cat out for the whole night. If that doesn't work, encourage your cat to sleep in your roommate's or kid's room. If all else fails, you may have to succumb to locking your cat in another room at night. Just make sure your cat has a nice, comfortable room with a litter box, toys, treats, and a soft bed. Hopefully you won't hear the cries for room release resonate through your door.

How do I stop my cat from begging for food at 5:45 A.M.?

First of all, resist all temptation to get up and feed your cat. How do you think your cat figured out that you're a big enough sucker to get up to feed Fatty in the first place? Don't start this habit. My vet school housemate's cat woke her up every morning at 5 A.M. by screaming, howling, and begging for food; my housemate's response was to promptly get up, feed Crystal, and then go back to bed. It wasn't an issue for me, because I closed my bedroom door; however, when it was my turn to pet-sit, I quickly taught Crystal through negative reinforcement that this just wasn't going to happen while she was under my watch. Don't get me wrong, Crystal tried hard, but I ignored her crying and annoying ability to knock the phone off the night table so the beeping would drive me insane. After a few "gentle reminders" to get her off my head and some squirts of water with my new handy Super Soaker (don't go to bed without one, folks), she quickly learned that Justine doesn't wake up until Justine wants to wake up.

Why do some cats cover their poop but others don't?

When you adopt that cute kitten, you might think that Clumpin' Clayton naturally knows what to do in that kitty litter box, but think again. While *you* may not remember your potty training days, I'm sure your mother does. When Seamus was a kitten, I placed him in the litter box, gently grabbed his front legs, and showed him how to scratch and shovel in the box. While it sounds silly, I didn't want to risk being one of "those" owners with a cat that didn't cover up.

It's the equivalent of not flushing, and it dramatically increases the stink in your house.

Of course, wild lions and cats don't naturally use clumping litter. In the wild, dominant alpha cats would leave their feces exposed, as a reminder of who's boss. Submissive wildcats would cover their feces to hide their presence. Nowadays, most domesticated cats cover up their poop because they are fastidiously clean, while others may or may not as an act of dominance (or, I believe, laziness). If your litter box is too filthy, Clayton may also decide not to cover up, as it's too full and there's no extra litter to splash around without getting his paws dirty in the process. Thankfully, most domesticated cats instinctually figure out how to cover their poop quickly, but just to be on the safe side, show them how if you have them as a kitten. Now, if only we could teach them to poop in the toilet, put down the cover, and flush, it'd be an ideal world.

Does my cat recognize herself in the mirror?

Being a scientist, I decided to perform an animal experiment with my own cats (don't worry, folks, no animals were harmed in the process), so I took Seamus and Echo into the bathroom to see if they recognized their own reflection in the mirror. Based on this, I'd say most cats don't care about their reflection in the mirror—they quickly figure out that it's themselves and aren't scared of the image. I've heard of kittens playing with their reflection for a few minutes, but they quickly lose interest and figure it out once the "other kitten" seems to know all their moves, so it becomes pretty boring. Since animals are sensory dependent, they rely on multiple senses: a combination of sight, smell, hearing, and potentially taste, before they know it's legit. This is also why your cat doesn't attack a picture of a goldfish or eat the Pounce ad in the paper.

What's the best way to hold a cat?

In general, most cats don't want to be carried or held too long. Cats want to feel secure when you are holding them, so make sure to support their (often big, at least for Seamus) bottom while also using your other hand to hold their chest area close to you. Most cats don't want to be picked up with one hand and generally don't appreciate being lifted by the belly. Echo, who is a slim, muscular cat, is the exception: he likes to leap up while I'm typing, and with him, I can just swoop him up with one hand (which supports him between his front arms). I can easily position him onto my lap and he's in instant heaven. Of course, he's about half the size of Chub-chub (Seamus's nickname), so he's lighter to lift. Seamus, on the other hand, is so fat that I can barely lift him with one arm unless I start my New Year's resolution of doing twenty biceps curls a day. Seamus would feel really insecure dangling in the air in a one-hand stance so I have to lift him with two hands to distribute the weight and make him feel more balanced.

Once you lift your cat, don't cradle him like a baby (with his belly exposed)—cats generally resent having to show you their chubby belly, as they feel more vulnerable this way. Since cats like to be on top of the world, they may prefer the baby hold over the shoulder, where they can rest their front legs on your shoulder, scope around, and still have you supporting their weight. Finally, all things in moderation, particularly when it comes to cats. Go slowly. If you just adopted a newly socialized (formerly feral) cat, he won't want any immediate human affection. Cuddle your cat for short increments, and then immediately give him a treat. That way, he'll see that hugs and nice touches aren't so bad, after all.

My favorite childhood picture is of me at the age of two, holding my first kitten, MiMi, with her arms spread wide and her body held at uncomfortable angles in my arms. No wonder I have so many memories of cat scratches. Two decades later, when I adopted my kitten Seamus, I couldn't get him to "love" me. He just wasn't a well socialized or affectionate kitten, and never wanted to be held or touched. I had to host nightly "forced love" sessions with him, where I'd cuddle him for one minute and then put him down. Gradually, I tried increasing the session times, but he still never loved them. Guess that teaches me that you can't force love after all.

Since moving to Minnesota, however, and now that Seamus is middle-aged, he seems to like nightly affection. Of course, I shave him in late summer to decrease the shedding, and as soon as those cold autumn nights come around, Seamus craves cuddle time under the duvet covers. Despite his heat-seeking attempts to stay warm, Seamus seems to appreciate a good cuddling now that he's a mature cat, as long as he can call the shots and leave whenever he wants to.

Is it true that cats can "suck a baby's breath"?

You may notice Tigger hanging near the crib, as he is likely attracted to the weird smells of a sleeping baby, such as the sour milk that gets burped back up and drooled all over the baby, clothes, bib, and sheets. Since cats are curious, and female cats can be maternal, they may be attracted to the gentle whimpering or cooing of a baby and go over to the crib to check out the noise. Unfortunately, since cats were historically associated with the devil, witches, and everything bad (twelfth century, people! Let's move on!), folklore about a cat's sucking a baby's breath began. What likely happened was that a cat was found in a crib with a deceased baby, who had likely died of sudden infant death syndrome. Another medical explanation for cats' "sucking a baby's breath" would be if the baby had *severe* asthma, which was exacerbated by allergies to cats. During a severe asthma attack, bronchoconstriction (lung contraction) and difficulty breathing could occur, potentially resulting in death. This isn't the same thing as baby-breath "sucking." Since then, moms are paranoid that cats can suck a baby's breath out, causing them to die. Come on, folks—let's think about how small your cat's mouth is—do you really think it's possible for that tiny cat mouth to cover the mouth of a human infant and suck out its breath? Poor cats get blamed for everything.

Can cats really predict death or cancer?

In July of 2007, CNN and the *New England Journal of Medicine* made Oscar the cat famous. This two-year-old gray and white cat was the subject of an article called "A Day in the Life of Oscar the Cat," written by geriatrician Dr. David Dosa,[6] and later reported on by CNN. At a nursing home in Providence, Rhode Island, Oscar had the unusual ability to accurately predict death within a four-hour window. Typically an aloof loner, Oscar would curl up on a person's bed only when death was imminent. While it seemed morbid, the nurses and doctors were so amazed by his accuracy (having predicted twenty-five deaths, up to the time of his fame) that they would call family members to rush them in.

What we don't know is if cats, who have a strong sense of smell, can pick up on unusual chemical odors (from either cancer or imminent death) that we, as humans, can't detect. Maybe there are environmental factors that make it seem like cats can predict death; for example, terminally ill patients may have more heating pads and electronic monitoring devices (such as heart and blood pressure monitors), and the heat and soft buzzing of the machines may be soothing to cats. I'd like to think that we underestimate the amazing inner sense of cats, and while most veterinarians and cat lovers are aware of this, it's nice to see medical doctors, nurses, and CNN finally realize it too!

Is it true that cats usually run away to die?

Owners are usually shocked when I tell them that their cat has been sick for more than just "one day." While their cat may have only been showing clinical symptoms for one day, they have been masking their signs for days to weeks prior. Don't feel guilty. Cats don't show their signs until they are very severe, which makes it harder for us as owners and veterinarians to be able to detect or treat their problems. I always have to assure my clients that it wasn't anything they as owners "missed"; cats have simply evolved to mask their signs. No point in showing the predator that you're limping, dehydrated, and too weak to run away. Even wildcats, who are higher on the food chain, mask their signs so their competition doesn't take over too soon. Once they are ready to die, they wander off and hide. No point in making it too obvious for takeover.

If you notice Simba hiding, that's a classic sign that you should take him to a veterinarian immediately. If you even *think* that Simba is what we fondly call ADR (ain't doin' right), he is, and it's been going on for longer than you think. When in doubt, bring him to a veterinarian for a checkup and some blood tests. Their stoic nature demands immediate attention by you.

What's my cat's tail telling me?

If you notice your cat flicking his tail angrily from side to side with short, snapping motions, this is a sign that he's annoyed and doesn't like whatever you're doing. Take this as a sign to stop, or you may get a paw swap in the process (or even a bite). When I first adopted Echo, he was very shy and poorly socialized from having lived at the shelter for several years. He was mentally frustrated and confused; he wanted to be near me and would sit on my lap, but as soon as I touched him, I'd get the angry tail swishing. It took a few months, but he eventually learned through slow acclimation that nice touches are indeed *nice*.

If you notice your cat's tail *slowly* and gently wagging back and forth, it may indicate contentment (think of a cat lying in the sun on a porch). If the wagging is slightly more rapid (but not quite as fast as the angry tail snap), your cat may be curious and found something intriguing like a bug or bird to chase. If you just walked in the door, you may notice that your cat's tail is straight up—that's a sign he's happy to see you. If your cat just encountered a dog for the first time, he may have a bushy, fluffed-up tail, as he's trying to look intimidating and larger in size. This is a sign of fear, which may result in aggression.

Lastly, for all owners of unneutered male cats (or inappropriately urinating cats), if you notice your cat's tail raised straight up, and he's attempting to shake his booty by quivering his butt and tail up against a vertical surface, be prepared for some foul, strong-scented urine marking about eight inches above the floor, slowly dripping down your wall. You can avoid this problem by neutering your cat before six to nine months of age and making sure he has appropriate litter box habits (see "Why does my cat spray?" in chapter 9). At least he's giving you a five-second warning before you run screaming toward him like a banshee.

Do cats cause schizophrenia?

While we all know that cats are crazy, can they make *us* crazy? A few years ago, studies suggested that *Toxoplasma gondii,* a common parasite shed in cat feces (see "Do I have to get rid of my cat when I'm pregnant?" in chapter 9), may be linked to the development of schizophrenia.[7] While it's true that toxoplasmosis can cause miscarriages or "adversely affect fetal brain development,"[8] we're not positive if it is directly linked to schizophrenia. This study[9] found high levels of antibodies to *Toxoplasma* in blood samples (that had been frozen for thirty years) from pregnancies that resulted in sixty-three schizophrenics, while moderate levels of antibodies to *Toxoplasma* weren't statistically associated with schizophrenics. Unfortunately, despite the multiple studies out there, there's still not definitive proof that *Toxoplasma* directly causes this disease.[10] Families with a history of schizophrenia have a seven times higher likelihood of having it continue in their lineage, while other risk factors (such as leaded gasoline, high levels of interleukin-8, herpesvirus, rubella, urban settings, glutens, vitamin D deficiency, influenza, cytomegalovirus, painkillers, time of year, birthing intervals, and of course, *Toxoplasma*) have also been blamed.[11]

Chapter 5

TRAINING THE FOUR-LEGGED BEAST

WHY is it so hard to train cats? Dogs are so obedient—they crave that attention and mental stimulation. Cats? They don't care. They don't want to be obedient. They don't want the attention. And they could not care less about mental stimulation—after all, they are perfect as is. My dog is a puppy and intermediate class graduate and is now a well-trained, obedient pooch. With my cats, I *tried* to start off as a good owner. I even attempted harness training Seamus so I could teach him how to walk on a leash. That lasted about one month. Since then, I've given up on my cats. At least Seamus and Echo come when they're called (thanks to bribery with cat treats). Apparently, I've accidentally trained my cats to graciously allow me to live in *their* world.

So if this veterinarian fails to train her cats, what are you to do? What's the best way to persist in your cat training? Should you even bother teaching your cat tricks? Can you teach your cat to fetch? While we all know that you can teach an old dog new tricks, find out that the same is *not* true for cats, and it's not as easy as it looks. More important, read on to find out how can you train Tigger to do what you want, like bat the remote closer to you (yeah, right) or stop leaving dead creatures on your pillow.

What's Feliway and what does one do with these feline pheromones?

Notice how Toonces rubs his face all over you and your furniture? That's a sign that he's marking his territory and that he's content and happy in "his space." He's releasing his scent, or *pheromone,* which is produced from glands on his face (see "Why do cats rub their faces and bodies all over you, your furniture, and your houseguests?" in chapter 4). What you may not know is that now you can buy it in a bottle. (Thankfully, this idea hasn't caught on with men; otherwise bottled human pheromones would be the rage. Bathing in Drakkar is enough.) Feliway, an analogue of feline facial pheromones (try saying that three times fast!), is designed to help calm down Toonces. Don't worry—it doesn't have any kitty crack or illicit substances in it. It's used to soothe Toonces in a stressful environment or to help prevent urinary marking. Being that most cats don't usually handle stress well, a little chemical dependency isn't such a bad thing, right? If you're planning on putting Toonces in the cat carrier, moving into a new house, getting a new cat or dog, rearranging furniture, coming and going from the veterinarian, taking your suitcase out of the closet to prepare for vacation, or looking at Toonces cross-eyed (in other words, it doesn't take much to stress him out!), consider using some Feliway to mellow him out. Before using it, check with your veterinarian to make sure your cat isn't having medical problems that are causing him to urinate all over your house (like bladder stones or a urinary tract infection) or to otherwise act stressed out (like feline lower urinary tract disease—see "What is FLUTD and how do I treat it?" in chapter 2).

When using Feliway, carefully read the instructions first. You're not supposed to directly spray the pheromones on Toonces; instead, spray it on a piece of cloth and place it in the cat carrier. You can also spray it around prominent objects in your house (like basement corner walls or on surface corners of tables or chairs) to prevent your cat from urine marking (just color test a small hidden area of carpet first, or your walls may smell urine clean but be hideously stained). Hopefully, you'll find that it helps make Toonces more mellow. And no, it doesn't work on humans.

How should my cat's collar fit?

While working in Philadelphia, I had an owner frantically rush her cat to the ER. Her house had just been broken into, and she thought that the robber had cut her cat's neck, as there was a large, gaping, dripping wound there. Apparently, the frantic owner didn't notice the foul pus smell that had been lingering for days prior to the robbery. Upon closer inspection, her cat's collar had embedded through the skin, as it had been too tight for weeks, resulting in sloughing and rotting of the skin and neck. Thankfully, after surgery, the cat recovered just fine. Unfortunately, the owner had two traumatic events that night, both of which cost her some dough. When you place a collar on your new, growing kitten, make sure to adjust it at least once a week as Kitty grows into the new collar.

Another time, I had an owner rush his cat in for acute neurologic signs: his cat was hanging his neck at an abnormal angle with his mouth wide open. He was convinced this was all caused by rabies or a brain tumor, and was very devastated. After $150, I gently removed his cat's collar from the lower jaw and teeth. Apparently, while grooming, his cat's new, loose, fuzzy collar got stuck around the jaw, trapping his cat's head at an awkward angle.

Learn from these poor people who had to pay an ER fee: make sure your cat's collar fits appropriately—not too tight, not too loose, but with just enough room to stick one or two fingers through. That advice, my cat lovers, is free.

Can I train my cat to walk on a leash or body harness?

One of my favorite patients, Ulysses, was a beautiful Burmese cat who walked around the hospital on a leash. Despite barking dogs or towering two-legged humans quickly scurrying about, Ulysses calmly strutted around as if he owned the world. His owner had trained him to walk on a harness and leash since he was a kitten, and he went outside for a walk twice a day (which is the safest way to let your cat outside—supervised, leashed, and well trained!). In fact, Ulysses came when called and ran over enthusiastically to slip into his harness.

Cats can learn how to walk on a leash, but don't be fooled: if you've never tried this before, know that it's not as easy as it looks. I tried to train Seamus as a kitten but had a hard time getting him adjusted to his harness—he'd roll around and "bunny kick," as we veterinarians so fondly call it, using his back legs to claw at anything near him to try to get it off. Unfortunately, leash time just became "freeze-up-and-get-dragged" time, so neither of my cats is leash trained now. If you want to impress your friends and your veterinarian, train your kitten *early* with gentle persistence.

When starting with a harness, make sure it is snug and has your cat's identification information on it. Practice inside the house first, before adding in any outdoor distractions. Once your cat is used to the harness, attach a short leash to it, so he gets used to having the tension of a leash behind him. Make sure to always closely supervise your cat while he has a leash on, as you don't want him to get tangled up. When he gets used to the harness, start walking him on the leash in short intervals, gradually increasing the duration. Before you know it, you may have a Ulysses-on-a-leash, strutting his stuff down the sidewalk.

How do I prevent Twinkie from killing small, innocent creatures?

Cats are natural predators so don't be surprised when your cute, fluffy, beautiful Twinkie stalks and kills songbirds and chipmunks. Regardless of your attempts to quash his outdoor murdering spree, you may not be able to stop his innate hunting desire to kill the neighborhood chipmunks, squirrels, baby rabbits, or small rodents. Because cats are the number one killer of songbirds in North America, we veterinarians are advocates of keeping cats indoors: this is the only way for you to truly prevent Twinkie from killing small creatures (see "How many songbirds do cats kill a year?" in chapter 7).

If you've tried and tried and still can't convert Twinkie to the great indoors, then try supervising him while outside. After all, you wouldn't let your two-legged kid play outside without watching him like a hawk, right? Try keeping him in a fenced-in yard that he can't jump or burrow out of, or otherwise escape from, or supervise him on a leash and harness. Consider adding on a quick-release collar with a bell. The quick-release collar will prevent accidental strangulation (if the collar gets stuck on a tree branch), while the bell will function to give some warning to the poor bird or chipmunk. When in doubt, add on a brightly colored CatBib, which is a neoprene, lightweight, easy-to-clean barrier (in case it doesn't work, you need to be able to wash off all the bird blood) that you attach to your cat's collar. The CatBib is large enough that it acts as a physical barrier to prevent Twinkie from getting to whatever rodent or bird he's trying to maim and bright enough to scare even humans away. Proven to reduce deaths by 50 percent, it's worth considering to save those other critters in your yard. Last, you can always use a designated cat fence. Though your neighbors might think you strange, you can help limit the access Twinkie has to the great outdoors, while still providing him with lots of sunlight, exercise, fresh air, and grass to chew on while in the safety of your giant net (see Resources).

Why does Tigger torture small creatures prior to killing them?

Tigger likes to torture small creatures for several reasons. He's not killing prey because he's hungry (as chances are you're already feeding him way too much). Being a natural-born killer, he has strong predatorial instincts that are hard to stifle, and playing with that daddy longlegs or mouse is so much more fun once it has been partially maimed. That way, Tigger gets more bang for his buck—not only does he get to do some chewing, but he can play with it longer to maximize his prey fetish. Being a creature of curiosity that's driven by motion, Tigger's prey instinct is triggered when that poor, wounded creature still moves around, stimulating Tigger to attack it over and over again (hence the saying "playing cat and mouse"). Apparently, it's just more fun to render that small creature unconscious, chew on a leg, then bat it around some more once it comes to—only to kill it fifteen minutes later. It's the feline equivalent of the lunch buffet that has free refills. Gross.

How do I prevent my cat from bringing in dead animals and leaving them on my bed?

Nothing's worse than waking up in the middle of the night, reaching over to pet your cat, and finding a half-dead mouse lying on your pillow instead. Aghhhhh! If *that* doesn't convert you to making your cat an indoor cat, no amount of veterinary encouragement and spewing of feline longevity statistics will. Honestly, there's not much you can do about his predatorial nature. No amount of your parental negative reinforcement will work, as it's an intuitive, innate instinct. You can, however, view the dead bird or mouse on your bed as a sacrifice or gift of love, and you should be honored that your cat wants to show it off to you. Humans aren't very good at sharing, so perhaps we can learn a thing or two from our cats.

How do I train my cat from getting stuck in trees?

Owing to their curious but "I don't know when to turn back around" nature, cats will chase after whatever was going up the tree but lose their sense of propriety and not realize that they may have gone just a bit too far. So, yes, cats can easily climb *up* trees; it's the going back down thing that they haven't figured out. Luckily, we have firefighters to help rescue our feline friends in desperate situations! Unfortunately, the only ways you can train your cat *not* to get stuck in a tree are to (a) keep him indoors, (b) let him outdoors but only while supervised on a leash to avoid annoying your local fire station, (c) trim his nails frequently so his nubbins are nice and dull and he can't climb that high to begin with, or (d) pry him off the base of the tree trunk as a kitten and reverse his direction so he learns to climb back down. Your safest options are the first two.

How can I make my antisocial cat more social?

Depending on your Myers-Briggs Type indicator personality, would you like someone to force you to convert from an introvert to an extrovert? Probably not. That said, don't give up—you may be able to slowly convert your cat from a loner to a lover. Remember, cats are like men. With appropriate behavioral modification, even an anti-PDA boyfriend can learn how to hold hands in public. All in moderation. And with patience. And Pounce treats. So while it seems impossible, be gently persistent.

Keep in mind that cats, like dogs, humans, horses, and any other random species out there, have different personalities. It may be that you just own an aloof cat. If you're about to buy a purebred cat, and want a jovial, outgoing Paris Hilton socialite, realize that there may be some breed variety, so do your research first. For example, Siamese and Maine Coons are particularly friendly. If you're adopting from a shelter situation (good owner), I find long-haired gray cats particularly shy, while orange and white tabby males seem to be the friendliest (see "Why are orange tabbies almost always male while calicos and tortoiseshells are always female?" in chapter 1). Of course, don't judge on color alone; just take this as a word to the wise.

If Skidway, your newly adopted cat, is skittish, start slowly. If you've given him plenty of time to acclimate to your house, and he still runs away from you, try making less noise. In other words, heavy footsteps running down the stairs may scare him away, and so gentle, slower movements toward him may help. If you have Skidway's kitty litter and food tucked away into the dark, damp corner of the basement, try slowly moving his food to an area that is low-traffic but more social (such as in a quiet corner of the kitchen or dining room). Begin by placing his toys, treats, and cat house in a peripheral area of the room that you mostly frequently inhabit. A quiet area under the table may offer him some more security, while allowing him to survey the entire room (in case you decide to attack him with some canned food when he least expects it). Once he starts branching out and showing his face, gradually (I mean *gradually*, as in weeks) move the toys and treats to a more central area of the room. Offer him irresistible toys such as, you know, a plain paper bag or cardboard box to hide and play in, and you may find that his inner scaredy-cat melts away. Try tempting him with his favorite treats (such as dollops of canned food) a few feet away from you while you're quietly vegging on the sofa. He'll start getting closer and closer, and before you know it he may soon be sitting on the arm of the sofa. Provide a plush fleece on top of the sofa for Skidway to lie on. When in doubt, try chemical bribery such as some catnip sprinkled on that blanket near you. In just a few weeks, he'll be lovin' you up on the sofa. Give Skidway a gentle, soft pat on the head or rub on the butt. As he gradually warms up to you, extend the time you pat him by just a few more seconds. After doing so, give him a dry kibble or a treat as a reward for tolerating you. Over several weeks, you'll have gotten him used to a few minutes of nice touches. Small baby steps, and before you know it, your little introvert may start hanging around you.

Why don't cats come when called?

Cats are aloof, fastidious, independent creatures who don't like to answer to anyone. Your cat can hear you calling her;

she just may not feel like answering. That said, don't give up. With appropriate training, your cat may soon recognize her name and come to you when called. If you want to train your cat to come to you when you call her, start by using a short name with a vowel at the end (like "Echo")—that'll make it easier for your cat to distinguish your daily gibberish and babbling from her name. Next, use positive reinforcement (i.e., bribery). When you're feeding her a canned food snack or a treat, call her name. Before you know it, she'll be running each time you holler. Seamus and Echo both come when called, thanks to years of bribery and reward. Whenever I call them, I always reward them with some type of treat: an ear scratching, a small piece of kibble, or a quick butt smack (the gentle kind). I also call them every evening for their nightly dollop of canned food grub (everyone should have a small pre-bedtime snack, right?). Makes it easier to train them to come get their medication too, if that day ever comes. For all you dog types, don't get frustrated with your cat when it comes to training. Remember, dogs generally like to please their master and be obedient. Cats don't care, and it's OK to use bribery instead.

Can I teach my cat tricks?

How many obedience or agility trained cats do you see out there? No matter how much Animal Planet you watch, know that those agility cats are in the minority. While we have "domesticated" cats, we haven't taught them to obey verbal commands to the extent that dogs do. Dogs were originally bred for function: to hunt, fetch, retrieve, and to obey. If you were relying on a duck hunt for food, and your dog ran off with your meal for the night, he'd be out in the doghouse. Likewise, if you were relying on your Saluki to catch you a rabbit for your next meal, you'd start breeding dogs that were functional—fast, obedient, voice responsive, and over-all good hunters. Since then, dogs have evolved to respond to humans in a reciprocal relationship—we feed and care for them; they listen and love us back in return. Cats, on the other hand, think it's a one-way street. They expect us to love them, feed them, clean their litter box, and care for them, but they're too dignified to have to do it based on "re-ward." (Little do they know . . .) It's not that cats aren't smart enough (they may be *too* smart); it's just that they don't see the point of behavioral modification ("What's it going to get me?").

The exceptional, rare cat will do tricks for his owner, but it takes extensive training to get Kitty Copperfield to perform of his own accord. If you want to make your cat a Copper-field, start with a treat that he can't resist (regular dry kibble isn't going to cut it). Only train for three to five minutes at a time, as he'll quickly (a) get bored or (b) get sick of too much "you" time. Second, be consistent. If you only "train" once a week, you're not going to hammer this new trick into his brain. Short, consistent training sessions are best, for three to five minutes, once a day for weeks at a time, until Copperfield gets it. If that doesn't work, give up (I'm not a pessimist; I'm just a realist)—can't-be-Copperfield just doesn't care to learn your dumb human trick. I tried to train Seamus to do tricks but failed miserably. His one trick is to fetch crumpled dollar bills, and he'll drop the crumpled ball by my feet so I throw it over and over again; of course, Sea-mus had severe head trauma as a kitten and kind of acts like a dog at times too, but hey, I'll take what I can get. So I wouldn't say it's *impossible* to teach a cat tricks—it's just that the rest of the cat population is content making *you* work for *them*.

How do I exercise my fat, indoor cat?

Just like the warning label on an exercise bike advises you to consult your physician, always check with your veterinarian to make sure that it's safe for Chunky Charlie to be starting a rigorous exercise program (see "What's my cat's ideal weight?" in chapter 6). Chances are, yes, we'll validate his requirement for some calorie cutting and exercise, but we want to examine him first and make sure he's healthy otherwise and doesn't have a heart murmur or other metabolic conditions.

Start exercising Chunky for a few minutes a day. Make sure to purchase entertaining, fun toys such as furry fake mice, bells in fleece balls, feather-on-a-rope toys, or anything that gets Chunky moving. Just make sure the toys are safe: no string or pieces of plastic that Charlie could swallow, or no lead-coated toys from China. Remember, variety is the spice of life in the cat world, so mix it up frequently. Try a small laser pointer to have him chase the red beam around; of course, this will only last a few minutes before he'll get bored by it, but you'll take whatever movement you can from Chunky Charlie. Buy some catnip to stuff into a mouse toy, and encourage Chunky to chase and play with it. Try attaching a thick piece of yarn and feather to your waist pocket while you're running around and cleaning the house—that'll encourage Chunky to chase furiously after you (provided he's not attacking your leg or ankle). Finally, try not to use snacks or food as a constant treat, as you're trying to help him lose weight here, right? Ideally, try not to feed him right before exercising, so Chunky doesn't feel full and nauseated while exercising.

Some cats like cheap toys, like an empty paper bag, a large cardboard box, or balled-up pieces of paper. Seamus loves chasing pieces of paper, although he seems to have expensive taste—he prefers wadded-up dollar bills over paper. When I moved out of my apartment, I was embarrassed when the movers came to lift the sofa; over fifty pieces of wadded-up paper were sitting just out of the cat's reach under the sofa. Hey, it's cheap, easy, and entertaining for your cat, right?

Why does my cat suddenly break out in sprints, like he's training for the Olympic 200-meter race?

Poor Tigger. He actually thinks he's a cheetah, sprinting off at seventy miles per hour to go chase down his dinner. Tigger still has lots of pent-up energy from his old predatorial days, as he doesn't actually have to worry about where his next meal is coming from. Tigger might also be plain bored. Just like how we get stir-crazy sitting around on a cloudy, rainy, cold day indoors, so does Tigger. His wind sprints are a fun way for him to let it all out. Get the hint, and help exercise and entertain him a bit more.

Why does my cat knock things off my countertops?

Ever notice that if you're ignoring your Persian, she'll purposely start doing things to make you notice her? Principessa wants all the attention and might start batting things off the table with her paw to conveniently "play." Did you like that vase?

Of course, we cat owners know that while the animal behaviorists *say* cats aren't *purposely* vengeful, they probably don't own cats. If I'm gone for a few days on business, I often come home to a trashed house with papers and junk all over the floor. Chances are, my cats weren't deliberately or purposely trying to get revenge. Seamus and Echo likely just made the mess while they were playing, as they were probably (very) bored while I was gone. I'm sure my beeper, that crumpled piece of scrap paper, and that paper clip looked like very appealing, fun toys. After all, they're just trying to have fun, Mom.

More important, depending on how often you Clorox, it's not that healthy to have Principessa on your countertops and dinner table. Remember where her paws have been? The dusty kitty litter footprints should be a gentle reminder . . . Because of the risk of bacteria or toxoplasmosis spread through fecal-oral contact, it's best to keep her paws off counters, stovetops, and tables. If you want to keep your cats off the countertops, try these hints. First of all, be a neat freak. The less crap there is on your counters, the less there is for Principessa to investigate. As long as you don't have friends, family, or guests over, apply (lots of) double-sided tape on the countertop. Not only will it help trap dust and dirt so you have to clean less (yeah, right), but when your cat jumps up, she'll quickly learn that having her lovely paws stuck to the counter isn't very fun. If you don't mind having your house looking like you're an alcoholic, you can also put empty aluminum beer cans on the edge of the counter (just toss a few coins inside so they rattle with any movement); that way, when your cat jumps up and knocks them down in-advertently, the loud noise will scare her and dissuade her from returning. If all else fails, use the Super Soaker water gun when you actually catch her in the act of walking on your counters. Then Principessa will just learn to do it when you're not at home.

Chapter 6
CATKINS DIET

AFTER the devastating and fatal pet food scare in March 2007 by Menu Foods, the pet food maker of almost 100 different types of dog or cat food, dozens of animals were killed, with cats being more severely affected. Because of melamine exposure (a chemical used in plastic, glue, fertilizer, and cleaning products), over 60 million pouches and cans of pet food were recalled, along with several million pounds of dry kibble.[1] Turns out that the wheat gluten from China (along with rice protein and possibly corn gluten from South Africa) was "contaminated" or "adulterated."[2] While this hasn't been confirmed, the U.S. Food and Drug Administration (FDA) and veterinary nutritionists were concerned that this was done in an attempt to falsely increase the "protein content" of the food when it was scientifically analyzed for content. For protein content analysis, the amount of nitrogen equates to how much protein there is, and unfortunately China's addition of melamine was a cheap but deadly way of supplying nitrogen without the nutritional benefit of any real protein. In fact, the melamine and a melamine-related compound, cyanuric acid, resulted in crystal formation in the tubules of the kidneys, resulting in severe kidney failure.[3]

Unfortunately, we're not sure of the total "official" number of deaths from this massive recall. The Veterinary Information Network, which is a vet resource that more than half of the practicing small-animal vets in America belong to, conducted a survey that suggested that vets saw between 2,000 and 7,000 pet deaths[4] from contaminated food—but we're not sure if this included the immeasurable number of affected animals that may never have been reported. The FDA reported over 18,000 complaints, with approximately a quarter of those calls reporting deaths of a pet.[5] I personally only saw a handful of cases, but they were heartbreaking nevertheless. I'm afraid we'll never know the true damage that this nightmare food recall caused.

Since then, owners have been justifiably scared to feed their cats, fearing life-threatening kidney failure as a result. We veterinarians have had an influx of owners who want to cook for their cats or want to change their diet completely. Is this for the best? I can barely cook for myself so wouldn't even attempt to cook for three more mouths (and twelve extra paws). What exactly is in cat food anyway? Should you make your cat a vegetarian instead? The answer is no, and in case you didn't know that, read on to find out how cats have such a unique digestive system.

Recently lost a lot of weight through the Atkins diet? Think it'll work on your chunky cat? Read on to find out if there's such a thing as the Catkins diet, and whether or not it's safe for your cat. With America's obsession with dieting, cat owners want to know what's best for their fat friend. This chapter tells you if Fluffy is trying to lose weight by becoming bulimic or anorexic like the Hollywood stars. Find out what your cat's ideal weight should be and how to go about achieving it. When it comes down to it, we cat owners have it easier than dog owners. After all, our cats don't eat their own poop, as only drooling, dirty dogs do. While it's a dog-eat-dog world, find out why Finicky Fluffy can't be starved out of stubbornness.

What's my cat's ideal weight?

The perfect or ideal weight of a cat is when they have a waist when viewed from the side. No potbellies allowed! When viewing your cat from above (stand over Chunky), if you see a pouching out behind the rib cage, it may be time for some weight loss. If you look at your cat's profile from the side, you should see an "abdominal tuck," not a large, dangling fat pad or pouch almost dragging on the ground. Finally, when you run your hands on both sides of your cat's chest, you should be able to feel the bones of the ribs just underneath the skin. Chances are you're feeling an abundance of skin (i.e., fat), right? Check out the Purina cat website (see Resources) to see what your cat's ideal weight should be.

My cat is overweight. What should I do?

It depends. Do you mind giving your cat insulin shots twice a day for the rest of his or her life, interspersed with expensive veterinary examinations?

Obesity is associated with a higher incidence and predisposition to diabetes, arthritis, and breathing difficulty, as well as more strain on the heart, trachea, lungs, and musculoskeletal system. More than 25 to 34 percent (and as high as 70 percent) of household pets are obese in America, meaning they are 20 percent heavier than their ideal body weight.[6] While this may not be on the top of your "to do" list, it should be. When your veterinarian tells you your cat needs to lose two to three pounds, it doesn't sound like a lot, but in actuality, it is. That's approximately 20 percent of your cat's overall body weight to begin with, and it's the equivalent of your doctor telling you to lose twenty pounds (think about the ratio of body size to weight). Based on the "fatness" of America, I can easily tell all of you readers to feed your cat 30 percent less without a second thought (providing your cat is completely healthy). Check with your veterinarian to make sure that your cat is on an appropriate amount of food (a low-fat, senior, high-fiber dry diet if necessary) and on a good exercise program (see "How do I exercise my fat, indoor cat?" in chapter 5).

Indoor cats are less active, so by increasing their exercise, you can help your cat get to his ideal weight. Entice your inactive "I'm not moving out of this sunbeam" cat by having him chase toys, laser pointers, or even another cat in the house. Consider decreasing the amount you are currently feeding your cat by at least a third. Break up your cat's meals into smaller, more frequent meals (once a day converted to three times a day); this may make your cat feel more full and help minimize begging. This does *not* mean feeding your cat three times more. Use an actual measuring cup to figure out the appropriate caloric intake for your cat's *ideal weight*. While it seems minuscule, a quarter cup twice a day may be all that your cat needs. As you near the bottom third of the bag of cat food, *gradually* mix in a senior or lower calorie cat food. It doesn't matter if your cat is only middle-aged—that extra fiber and lower calorie food may help him shed a few pounds. When in doubt, consult with a veterinary nutritionist or your vet for more information.

More recently, scientists have found that if you exercise with your pet, you *both* lose weight. Unfortunately, they were talking about dogs here (with the average dog and human losing about eleven pounds). As we don't jog around the block with our cats, this doesn't help us. Don't give up, though! We cat owners can only do so much when it comes to exercise. Regardless, you should still try. I leave my cat food in the basement, so Seamus and Echo have a few extra steps to take before gorging. I also exercise them with a laser pointer. I know it's not much, but remember, I've a veterinarian, and I feel much more comfortable giving insulin shots.

Is the Catkins diet like the Atkins diet?

Some cats are so fat that they can't even turn around to groom themselves and end up having dingle berries (fecal balls) stuck to their back fur. Do you really want to subject your poor cat to that? Just like in human medicine, we veterinarians see a lot of obesity in our pets today. I've had a lot of clients who tell me that their veterinarian said that Kitty was in perfect body condition and then get offended when I tell them that Kitty is obese (making me look like the bad guy). Veterinary students think I'm a hard-ass and quiver when I reprimand them for calling a pet's body condition "normal" ("Dude! He's obese!"). Some veterinary students graduate from school and are so used to seeing overweight animals that they can't identify a perfectly conditioned animal, which is rare nowadays. I want my clients and students to realize how overweight their cat is so we can move on and fix the problem. While two to three pounds overweight doesn't sound like much, that could be 20 to 30 percent of Kitty's ideal body weight (they're only supposed to be eight to ten pounds to begin with, you know).

Weight loss for cats can take a lot of dedication and persistence as an owner (between the diet change, begging and crying for food, and your attempts at exercising your cat). Work with your veterinarian to discuss two options: feeding a high-fiber, low-calorie, low-fat diet (the traditional way), or feeding the Catkins diet: a high-protein, low-carbohydrate diet (as digesting protein takes more energy and calories). This diet is very similar to the Atkins diet—it's basically a high-protein-diet gorge fest. Keep in mind that humans, however, were meant to be omnivores, while cats were meant to be completely carnivorous and require a high-protein diet to begin with. If you decide to feed the Catkins diet, you have to feed an *extra*-high-protein diet that is only found in certain brands of cat food (such as Science Diet's *canned* kitten food) or prescription foods (such as Purina's D/M diet). What's important to note is that if you decide to feed your cat the Catkins diet, your cat may think he's died and gone to heaven. (What? Kitten canned food for the rest of my life? Score!) Also, know that *dry* kitten food doesn't even have enough protein to truly qualify for the Catkins diet, so you'd have to switch completely to Science Diet canned kitten food.

However, the Catkins diet has a few drawbacks—it's not as easy as it sounds. First, if you are feeding canned food once to twice a day, you definitely need a pet-sitter to come by twice a day if you go on vacation. Second, you have to buy canned food from now on, which is more expensive and is also messy, stinky, more environmentally unfriendly (even if you *are* recycling the cans), and higher maintenance. Third, you can't switch back and forth between canned and dry food—you have to be consistent, or Kitty will continue to pack on the pounds. Finally, it's important to work with your vet to make sure your cat is slowly acclimated to this diet so he doesn't become anorexic or lose his appetite (which can result in severe liver problems such as hepatic lipidosis or fatty infiltration of the liver). If your cat has underlying diseases (like kidney failure or intestinal problems), he may not be able to handle a high-protein diet. This Catkins diet could actually make his diseases worse! Consult your veterinarian before even thinking about the Catkins diet. Finally, regardless of which diet plan you pick for Kitty, have your veterinarian calculate the *exact* amount of resting energy requirements (RER) that your cat needs. Ideally, feeding 80 percent of the RER is a good place to start. Your ultimate goal for weight loss in a healthy, metabolically stable cat is 1 to 2 percent of current body weight per week. Alternatively, your long-term goal for your cat is to allow him to be able to clean his own butt again and to be dingle berry–free.

Is obesity expensive?

We all know that obesity in human health care is expensive, but did you know it's also expensive in veterinary medicine? With the growing problem of obesity, veterinary pet insurance companies are finding that obesity is pricey: for you, your pet, your vet, and the insurance companies. Last year, Veterinary Pet Insurance reimbursed owners for more than $14 million in weight-related issues. While you may be excited to be getting that money back, remember that Big Brother is always watching, and your fat cat is fleecing the likelihood that they'll start covering obesity, since it's usually owner induced. Medical problems such as hepatic lipidosis (fat infiltration of the liver), diabetes mellitus, pancreatitis, urinary tract infections, constipation, orthopedic problems, and asthma are all made worse by obesity, so it's important to trim that tummy off Kitty. Research studies have shown that both skinnier humans and dogs live longer, as they aren't as predisposed to all those extra problems from obesity. While there aren't current studies to show the same in cats, we suspect it's true. Trim off those extra pounds!

Can I give my cat milk?

No matter how much you think you're spoiling your cat by giving her some milk, beware: there's a small population of cats that are lactose intolerant. Lactose intolerance is an inherited trait, and since you don't know whether or not your cat is lactose intolerant or has a food allergy, it's always safest not to give your cat milk. I'll admit it: I spoil my cats and let them lick the ice cream bowl or sip the remaining milk in the cereal bowl on occasion. (Do as I say, not as I do.) If you're an astute enough owner to start noticing diarrhea in the litter box around the same time you gave your cat some milk, he's likely lactose intolerant, so stop the midnight ice-cream binges. Otherwise, you're probably pretty safe giving a *small* amount of milk as an occasional snack.

Why do cats eat grass?

Cats are strict carnivores and require an all-animal protein diet in order to get their essential amino acids (this type of amino acid or protein has to be obtained in the diet, as a cat's body can't make it on its own). So why is it that as soon as you let your cat outside, he runs for some grass to chew on? Unfortunately, this answer eludes even the smartest of veterinarians. I truly believe that sometimes cats just have a craving for veggies, the way we might after eating out for a week. Or it could be that your cat's stomach is slightly upset, and he purposely chews on grass to make himself vomit (after all, we all feel better after puking, right?). Lastly, some cats eat grass because they just plain like the variety of feeling a different texture in their mouth.

How can I make my cat stop binge eating?

Some cats will eat so fast and gorge that they irritate their stomach and immediately vomit it back up, star- and kibble-shapes intact. Seamus does this occasionally, but luckily Echo eats it back up, minimizing my cleanup. If your cat does this, try decreasing the amount that you are feeding him at once and split it into multiple meals. If that doesn't work, try putting the kibble in a more shallow, flat dog bowl—that way he can't eat quite as fast if the kibble is all spread out (that doesn't mean to put more food in that bigger bowl!). Another option is to put a big rock at the bottom of the bowl, so he has to slowly eat around the rock, slowing down his gorging and purging (hopefully).

If your cat is still vomiting more than once or twice a month immediately after eating, you can consider gradually changing him to a hair ball diet, which contains more fiber. If that doesn't work, a veterinary exam is a must! I'm often amazed how owners tolerate long-term vomiting: folks, it's abnormal to vomit that much, and something else may be going on.

Can I make my cat a vegetarian?

Harping on the topic yet again: dogs are omnivores while cats are *strict* carnivores. While there are cat vegetarian and vegan diets commercially available, these are *not* recommended by veterinarians. Please don't make your cat a vegetarian. If you want to cook for your cat (and can deal with having meat in your vegan refrigerator), then that's OK, as long as you realize that it is very difficult to make a homemade, nutritionally balanced diet for your cat without screwing something up. If you want to try it, make sure it's recommended by a board-certified veterinary nutritionist (that does not mean trying whatever you stumble upon on the Internet!). Without appropriate supplementation, cats that are fed vegetarian or vegan diets are at high risk for life-threatening deficiencies in amino acids and vitamins (i.e., lysine, tryptophan, vitamin A, and taurine deficiency), which results in severe heart dilation, congestive heart failure, and even blindness. Not worth the fatal risk.

Is canned food *really* bad?

Feel like most of your paycheck is going toward kitty litter and canned food? Is it worth dishing out the extra dough for canned food? While canned food itself isn't "bad," remember that you're basically paying for 70 percent water. Seamus and Echo's primary diet is dry food, which is what I recommend to my clients to help scrape away plaque and tartar when they chew the food. Truth be told, I do give Seamus and Echo a nightly tablespoon of watered-down canned food with a splash of omega-3 fatty acid oil each night. It's fish flavored, and I figured if fatty acids are good for me, it's good for them (there's actually a cat form, called Welactin).

When you first adopt your new cat, your initial introduction of food should be tough-love strict (i.e., dry food), as long as Kitty is eating (see "If my cat is being picky, can I just starve him until he eats?" in this chapter). If you offer dry food, chances are, your new humane society kitten will jump right in. If you start with canned food, semimoist food, or canned tuna, it'll be harder to get him to eat dry food down the line. Remember, if you feed your kid Honey Nut Cheerios, you'll never be able to switch back to just plain old Cheerios. Same goes for cats. For this reason, train Kitty to initially eat dry food.

I don't usually advocate canned food as a *primary* diet source alone except if warranted by certain medical conditions such as kidney failure, urinary tract problems (see "What is FLUTD and how do I treat it?" in chapter 2), and for the purposes of helping with the Catkins diet. It's been shown that cats stay more hydrated when eating canned food (again, it's 70 percent water), and it helps them drink and urinate more. If your cat has kidney or bladder problems, consult your veterinarian about adding in a canned food snack or even grueling it down with more water.

If my cat is being picky, can I just starve him until he eats?

Just ran out of your normal cat food? Had your hubby pick up the cheap stuff in the meantime? You may notice that Finicky Frankie doesn't want to touch the stuff. Is it OK to starve him until he eats? I mean, it works for dogs, so why won't it work for cats?

Cats are not small dogs and are very resistant to sudden change. You can't stubbornly starve cats just because you think they'll eat when they are hungry. In fact, cats can develop hepatic lipidosis, or fatty changes to their liver, within three to five days of not eating enough. When you notice that Finicky Frankie is lethargic, vomiting, hiding, showing general malaise, and that there's still plenty of cat food in his bowl, rush him to a veterinarian. You can also check for a subtle yellow color (jaundice) in the white of Finicky Frankie's eyes, or even on his ear tips. Often, by the time you as an owner notice it, Frankie's fluorescent. Untreated, hepatic lipidosis can lead to liver failure and clotting problems, so we need to treat it aggressively before it becomes life threatening. You'll have to spend more than $1,000 on an abdominal ultrasound and temporary feeding tube, so please, heed this advice and don't starve Frankie. You could have bought a lot more cat food for that!

Can people eat canned cat food?

When I was a child, I heard of poor senior citizens or home-less people surviving on canned cat food; however, when I became a veterinarian, I figured it was an old wives' tale told to children who didn't finish everything on their plate. Canned cat food is pretty similar to the cost of a can of tuna but tastes much worse, so I don't recommend it for human consumption. Cat food also has a much higher protein con-tent than what a human needs, so it's not a good choice for a Sunday evening dinner. Excess protein can result in more strain or work on your kidneys, so don't take the chance.

If I pay more for cat food, does it mean it's better?

In general, if you stick with a large, reputable, research-based pet food company, your cat's health is in good hands. Top brands include Science Diet, Iams or Eukanuba, and Purina. The Association of American Feed Control Officials monitors the nutritional content of animal food to ensure that diets are appropriately balanced for a particular species. Ingredients that are available for the pet food industry (i.e., what goes into your cat's bag of food) include human nonedible pet-food-grade by-products (parts of the animal that we don't normally eat such as tendons, cartilage, and organs) to human-grade ingredients (your filet mignon).

Unfortunately, the devastating pet food poisoning with melamine has made veterinarians, pet owners, and the pub-lic leery of pet food companies. It was frustrating that American-based companies were getting ingredients from other countries that didn't administer the same standard of quality control, and as a veterinarian and pet owner, I wasn't aware this was happening until it was too late. After having a cat come in with severe kidney failure (who was also temporarily blind from severe hypertension), and spending almost an hour counseling the guilt-stricken owner that it wasn't her fault, I went home one night teary-eyed and purged my own shelves. I ended up throwing away dozens of cans of cat food that were both expired and tainted. Thankfully, Seamus and Echo came out unscathed. After that experience, it made me really nervous about my cats' nutrition, but please know that 90 percent of the pet food industry wasn't affected by this recall—it's a few bad apples that ruin the barrel. On the contrary, I've had some dog owners switch to home-cooked or raw-food diets, and have had a few dogs in the past year die of severe complications to these new diets (like bones stuck in the esophagus to severe pancreatitis). Most of my cat owners are still sticking to their regular cat food, and we haven't seen any problems since then.

Keep all this in mind as you explore what's best to feed your cat. There are numerous cat forums out there on the Internet that discuss various breeds, diets, holistic medications, and medical opinions. Remember that everyone may have different opinions, and some of these sites provide very inaccurate information (there is no formaldehyde in cat food and no, once again, you can't make your cat a vegetarian). Make sure to research the topic carefully, and when in doubt, consult a veterinary nutritionist (see Resources).

Can I prepare a homemade diet for my cat?

Homemade diets can certainly be made for your *dog* for his or her specific needs (particularly for kidney failure, inflammatory bowel disease, liver disease, weight loss, or allergies) but homemade cat diets are often deficient in fat, energy density, and palatability (which is the result of substituting vegetable oil for fat). Homemade cat diets are rarely balanced, and even veterinary vitamin-mineral supplements may not be complete. Please consult a veterinary nutritionist before preparing a homemade diet for your cat. Yes, I know you can find veterinarians blogging out there on the Internet about how to make a homemade cat diet, but I'd really rely on the specialists of veterinary nutrition or internal medicine here. If you're interested in cooking, consider the book *Home-Prepared Dog & Cat Diets: The Healthful Alternative* by Dr. D. R. Strombeck,[7] a retired veterinary gastroenterologist from the University of California–Davis. He'll tell you the correct way of doing it!

Is it OK to feed my cat people food?

Seamus, Echo, and my dog, JP, get to split the leftover salmon skin off the grill, and they love it. The occasional tuna or chicken treat is fine for your cat, as long as your table food doesn't comprise more than 10 percent of your cat's daily intake. As cats have unique amino acid requirements, table food could be detrimental in large amounts. I once had an owner who fed her cat *only* canned tuna its whole life (ten years!). The severe mineral and amino acid deficiencies in this unbalanced diet caused the cat to go into heart failure. That's because the enzymes in an all-seafood diet (such as sardines, tuna, and salmon) break down important amino acids that result in taurine deficiency and secondary heart failure. If you're feeding seafood to your cat, always make sure to feed a balanced kibble approved by the Association of American Feed Control Officials along with it, which will help supplement those minerals and amino acids (see "If I pay more for cat food, does it mean it's better?" in this chapter).

There are also rare foods that can cause toxicity in our pets. For example, raisins and grapes are highly toxic to dogs. No one knows if they are toxic to cats yet, as scientists haven't force-fed any cats grapes to see if they develop secondary kidney failure. Most cats are picky and discriminating eaters and usually won't eat these non-meat-based treats. Regardless, don't take your chances, and avoid these two table snacks.

Since variety is the spice of life, people food *once in a while* is OK—as long as your cat doesn't have any underlying inflammatory bowel disease, underlying obesity, or other medical problems such as pancreatitis. Otherwise, stick to basic cat food, and only use people food as an occasional treat. After all, we weren't meant to eat Ben & Jerry's all day long either.

Why don't some cats like table food?

I know, I know. I just finished telling you not to feed your cat too much table food. But once in a while is OK. That said, maybe I just have the biggest food snobs ever, but I've noticed Seamus and Echo aren't big table food fans to the extent that JP is. Despite the offerings of tuna, chunks of salmon, or filet mignon leftovers, my cats just aren't always interested. They'll nibble on a few pieces, but generally get pretty bored with it. Luckily, JP stands by, ready to Hoover up whatever the cats leave behind. I know some clients whose cats are chowhounds, however, and will beg at the dinner table for Doritos, pasta, popcorn, or anything edible. Cats can be very picky when it comes to their diet and, being creatures of habit, probably don't like too much change. Your cat may just be content with the dry food, and if he doesn't like the table food offerings, that's OK.

Does canned food cause hyperthyroidism?

For the past two decades, rumor had it that feeding pop-top canned food (versus wet food that came in pouches) caused hyperthyroidism (see "What's hyperthyroidism?" in chapter 2).[8] Was it the chemicals or preservatives lining the can? Or was it exposure to flea sprays, powders, herbicides, fertilizers, or even simply living indoors that caused it? A study by C. B. Chastain and colleagues[9] showed that cats fed specific flavors (such as fish, liver, or giblet) of canned cat food had a higher incidence of hyperthyroidism owing to the high iodine content in the fish but found no correlation between hyperthyroidism and chemical exposure (to flea sprays and such). Another study showed that cats that sleep on the floor have a higher likelihood of being hyperthyroid too.[10] All these data are confusing, eh?

Should this make you not feed your cat canned food or let him sleep on the floor? Unfortunately, we scientists still aren't sure. What is important to consider are the multiple contributing factors when interpreting scientific studies. In other words, how are the statistics presented? Epidemiological data may be hard to interpret owing to the "human factor." For example, people who spoil their cat rotten (hey, nothing's wrong with that!) by feeding more canned food may notice that their cat is losing weight and developing signs of hyperthyroidism earlier than other owners. Does this mean that feeding canned food causes weight loss and hyperthyroidism? No! But what it *might* mean is that these same owners are willing to spend more money on canned food and are more inclined to bring their cat to a veterinarian sooner, thereby allowing their cat to be diagnosed with hyperthyroidism sooner. While I know it's confusing, the best option is to have your veterinarian help you interpret these weird statistics! So believe what you want, but know that I feed my cats salmon-flavored canned cat food as a periodic snack without fear of hyperthyroidism.

Why do some cats try to cover their food after eating?

Echo often "air buries" his canned food. By gently scraping his paw in the air around his food bowl, he attempts to bury the bowl so neither Seamus nor I can "see" it. Like mountain lions and wildcats, he's trying to save his treat for later. While he looks really cute doing it, this simulation of his ancestors' behaviors is, of course, ineffective since he can't actually hide his dish on the cold linoleum floor. This is also a trait we see in some dogs, who may "nose dig" around their food bowl, trying to save it for a rainy day.

Why does my cat like to chew on my hair?

Depends. What brand of shampoo and conditioner are you using? Some cats are attracted to the smell of your toiletries and may lick or chew on your wet head when you lie down to sleep. Seamus used to enjoy sucking the water out of my hair when I got out of the shower, but thankfully, he has given up this strange habit. Some cats chew on your wet hair because they think it's a new, fun source of water, while others may chew on hair as a sign of affection. If Aveda, your alley cat, is doing this, she may be grooming you as she would to another littermate. Being that your hair reminds her of her four-legged, long-lost relative's fur, it's what she'd prefer to lick. If it's excessive, just kindly remove Aveda off your pillow and shoo her away. If you try a more citrus-smelling shampoo, she may also leave you alone. Just know that cats don't care much about oral hygiene, and they're not chewing on hair in an attempt to floss their own teeth.

Chapter 7
THE GREAT INDOORS

I **ALWAYS** kept Seamus as an indoor cat, but recently I've started letting him outdoors into my fenced-in backyard, under careful supervision. He loves to run around and eat grass (only to puke it up minutes later, but thankfully, outside). However, once he started jumping the fence (with a frantic, mad vet running around the neighborhood, using her pit bull to help round him up), Seamus instantly lost his privileges and was condemned to the great indoors. While he still begs to go outside, I've decided to implement "tough love." I didn't trust that he'd be savvy enough to avoid cars, dogs, other people's attempts to adopt him, and the neighborhood brat, and I was fearful that he'd never find his way back.

So what's a cat owner to do about the great outdoors? Does Smokey beg at the back door for his opportunity to escape the blander (but safer) indoors? This chapter reviews all the hazards that exposing your cat to the great outdoors poses to him (and others), whether it's the safety of the birds in your bird bath, the other neighborhood cats, the neighborhood kid or dog (or coyote, depending on where you live), or those toxins sitting in your backyard (did you know that one leaf from the lilies in your garden could kill your cat?). Find out if it's worth letting Smokey outdoors all night to party with all the other nightlifers.

Do outdoor cats have more fun?

Let the statistics do the talking: the outdoor cat lives on average from two to five years of age, while the indoor cat lives to eighteen. So ultimately, it depends on how long you want to have your cat. Outdoor cats succumb to the "trauma of outdoor living," including all the bad things that we're trying to protect them from. As an emergency specialist, some of the top causes for presentation to the animal ER that I see include animal attacks (such as neighborhood dogs, feral cats, the neighborhood brat, coyotes, or even mountain lions), being hit by a car, poisonings (from antifreeze, rat poison, or toxic Easter lilies in the yard)—either intentional or accidental—and infectious diseases (such as feline immunodeficiency virus [FIV], feline leukemia [FeLV], and feline infectious peritonitis [FIP]—see "What are FIV and FeLV?" in chapter 2). And, as mentioned earlier, outdoor cats are the number one killer of songbirds in America.

While there's lots of controversy on this topic, most veterinarians generally don't recommend letting cats go outdoors. Despite what you think, cats can be just as content indoors. Making sure they have lots of toys, catnip, cat grass, and environmental stimulation or enrichment (like a human to play with) will keep them quite content. However, once cats have tasted the "great outdoors," it's very hard to keep them from crying for it, begging for it, or running out when that screen door opens. For that reason, it's always the safest approach to not even let your cat experience the great outdoors the first time.

If you do let your cat outdoors, please consult your veterinarian about appropriate vaccine protocols. We don't normally recommend that your cat get the FeLV vaccine unless your cat has potential exposure by going outside. That's because the vaccine isn't 100 percent effective and has very rare but potentially deadly side effects (like a cancer called fibrosarcoma at the site of injection). Also, if your cat has something infectious, please, please, please do not let him outdoors. If your cat has FeLV, FIV, or FIP, it's not fair and quite unethical to spread it to other cats in the neighborhood, as these diseases are highly contagious (via catfights and saliva or blood exchange). Likewise, if your cat is declawed, please don't let him outside. It's a dog-eat-dog world out there, and sending a declawed cat outdoors is like sending him to war without a gun. Finally, if you do let your cat outside, do not have a birdfeeder in your yard (a bit cruel, and I'll be forced to report you to the Sierra Club and the local SPCA!). More important, make sure that you add a collar, a microchip, and a bell to help prevent unnecessary cute-creature killings (Give those poor birds and chipmunks a warning, will you? See "How do I prevent Twinkie from killing small, innocent creatures?" in chapter 5).

Why do cats want to come right back inside when they just begged to go out?

Notice how Simba sits by the door, jumps and scratches at it, and then howls until you let him out, only to take two steps outside and want to come back in? It makes you almost want to leave him outside until he makes up his mind!

Well, you may have heard of cats chasing dogs and even

bears out of their yards. They mean business when it comes to fortifying their yard. Cats are very territorial and are very scent and smell oriented. When Simba goes out, he marks his territory by rubbing his scent glands all over (or worse, spraying his urine all over the yard). He wants everyone in the neighborhood to know that this yard is his. While it drives you nuts when he can't make up his mind if he wants in or out, he's doing this to check out the scene. With just a few sniffs, he knows if anyone's been out in his yard. Once he's confirmed this, Simba may prefer the comfort of the safer, warmer indoors. Just checking, Mom!

Why do cats make that weird guttural sound when they see a bird outside the window?

If you've been lucky, you may have heard the cough of a panther or snow leopard while at the zoo or while watching the Animal Planet network. This is their way of communicating instead of that typical cute, lovable meow. Likewise, your cat makes this rare bark when he sees something that he wants to catch. It's his excited, predatorial gurgle, indicating that he's ready to pounce. I've only seen my cats make this noise when they can't actually get to the creature outside (thanks to the safety of the window), and it may be their way of demonstrating their predatorial frustration. A cat normally wouldn't make a sound just prior to the pounce, as the noise would scare off their next meal.

How many songbirds do cats kill a year?

Just because I'm a veterinarian doesn't mean I love *only* dogs and cats. I'm a huge advocate for all species, and while I wouldn't own a bird again (that'll be explained in the third book), I still want birds to enjoy the splendors of flying and living in the great outdoors. Given that there are almost 80 million cats in the United States alone, if even one cat killed one bird a year, that's more than 80 million songbirds a year. Of course, many cats live indoors, so this hypothetical statistic isn't completely accurate. Still, if we assumed that a quarter of all cats in the United States had access to the great outdoors, that's over 20 million birds killed. That's not even including all those feral cats or those areas with a severe stray cat overpopulation (Europe, Asia). While there's no easy way for us to be able to accurately estimate how many songbirds are killed a year, cats are still suspected to be the number one killer.

Despite my telling you to add a bell to your cat's collar, it doesn't help as much as we hope, unfortunately. That's because cats are such good predators and are still astute at hunting noiselessly by slowly stalking their prey. While you may not love those boring starlings and bland sparrows, cats are actually responsible for also killing migratory nonnative species; after all, they're just passing through on their thousand-mile journey for a quick drink in your bird bath and aren't prepared for the cat predator. Check out the Point Reyes Bird Observatory website (see Resources) to learn about a great campaign on converting your outdoor cat to the indoors and helping save some birds in the process.

Is it safe to let my cat catch mice and squirrels?

Ideally, we don't want your cat killing wildlife, but hey—if it's to help reduce your basement's mouse population, then I'm OK with that. The concern is that uncommon diseases can be brought home by dead (or half-dead) creatures that your cat drags in, and while the likelihood of disease transmission is rare, it's still possible. Bacteria and even viruses (such as rabies, hantavirus, and tularemia) have been spread from rodents to humans. While the likelihood is pretty scarce (unless you live in the Southwest—Colorado, Arizona, or New Mexico—where it's more common), be careful picking up that carcass, as there is a chance you could get something horribly infectious from rodents.[1] Thankfully, rodents such as mice and squirrels don't commonly transmit rabies, as this virus kills these small hosts too quickly, denying them the time to propagate and spread the virus (by biting you or another animal) before they die. However, you don't want your cat brawling with or bringing home skunks, woodchucks, bats, and rabbits, as these animals are the most common carriers of the deadly rabies virus. When in doubt, keep your cat current on his or her rabies vaccine, especially if you have an outdoor feline, as you don't want him to turn into a rabies-infested, drooling mess.

Can I leave my cat outside on a leash?

While we already discussed training cats to walk on a leash or harness in chapter 5, please be smart about it. Always make sure to supervise your leashed cat outside, as you don't want to leave your cat neglected. I recently had owners bring their cat into the emergency room after they tied her outside on a long leash attached to a laundry line. The owners didn't think that Flying Fiona could reach the tree from her leash attachment, but she proved them wrong. Fiona ended up jumping for the tree branch, strangling and hanging herself off that branch, freaking out to the point that she made herself hyperthermic (to a temperature of 108°F, with 100°F being the norm), stressing herself out to the point that she had life-threatening low blood sugar and deprived herself of oxygen. When the owners found her several minutes later, she was almost unconscious, in shock, and panting. Luckily, Fiona ended up recovering well after a few days of intensive care and oxygen support (after a few thousand dollars), despite being neurologically impaired (almost brain dead) initially. If you are going to let your cat outside, let's be smart about it, folks!

What's a feral cat?

Sadly, a feral cat is a wild, unsocialized cat. Some may have initially been domesticated but may have lost their way and found a wild cat gang to live with instead. Often, it is very difficult to socialize a feral adult who has never experienced socialization with humans before. Feral kittens, however, have more hope, and can often be socialized if rescued early enough in age.

The average life span of feral cats is approximately two years of age, compared with the fifteen- to twenty-year-old indoor cat. Thanks to some rescue organizations where food and shelter are available, there are reports of feral cats living up to the age of twenty. Unfortunately, feral cats often succumb to diseases, predators, trauma, or even extreme environmental conditions (heat, cold weather, and starvation).

There are between 20 to 40 million feral cats in America (and even more worldwide) as a result of human neglect and irresponsibility. Thankfully, some rescue organizations trap feral cats to have them neutered and vaccinated, to help decrease pet overpopulation. If you notice a feral cat whose ear tip looks like it's been clipped off, it may have been trapped at some point in the cat's life and is now marked by some veterinarians as "Jiffy Lubed" (i.e., nail trimmed, neutered, dewormed, and vaccinated all at the same time).

Neutering or spaying your cat and keeping him or her

indoors is one of the best ways to decrease the cat overpopulation problem. Another way to help is to gently educate your friends who may have unfixed cats. Remember, all those intact, hormonal barn cats that are running around making more and more babies are very prolific, and before you know it you have a booming overpopulation of cats, as those babies are making more babies. Hosting a bake sale or a fundraiser to help defray the costs of spaying and neutering all those extra mousers, or offering to help find homes for the neutered kittens, may also help.

Can I get a "wild" housecat?

Domesticated cats evolved from wild feline species from Asia, Europe, Africa, Arabia, and India. While there is such huge variation in the wildcat species (just compare that huge Bengal tiger to a bobcat or mountain lion), we have only tamed or domesticated the small housecat. So where have the wild housecats gone? Some breeders have tried to reincarnate wild housecats by breeding our domesticated cat with the exotic wildcat, creating unique, wild-looking cat breeds such as the American Bobtail, Bengal, Bobcat hybrid, Desert Lynx, Highland Lynx, Ocicat, Pixie-bob, Savannah, Serval, or Serengeti. These cats range in size between a traditional housecat and a small bobcat and are still considered somewhat "wild," although some of these cats can adjust and become domesticated housecats. Most veterinarians don't recommend these breeds as housecats, as it's hard to breed out that wildness.

Domesticated housecats that have been rereleased into the great outdoors in urban or suburban areas may soon become "wild" or feral again. If these cats lose human contact and end up scavenging to survive, they may end up contributing to cat overpopulation and the spread of diseases. So whether you choose to buy a "wild" housecat or you find a feral cat, please know that they need lots of socialization, as it's hard to tame that wild side.

If I had the space, could I domesticate a tiger or wildcat?

Just because you have the space and money doesn't mean you should be housing wildcats or domesticated tigers. People have been obsessed with the prestige of owning a wild animal (dating back to royalty thousands of years ago and, more recently, to Michael Jackson). Breeders have recently started breeding wildcats such as the American Bobtail, Bengals, Bobcat hybrids, Ocicats, or Servals, and while they are beautiful, wild-looking cats, they aren't recommended as routine pets. Some of these cats are easy to handle, while some are wilder in nature.

If Michael Jackson can't afford the upkeep and care for his two Bengal tigers, Thriller and Sabu, what makes you think that you can? Thankfully, they were adopted by Melanie Griffith's mom, Tippi Hedren, who happens to come attached to Dr. Martin Dinnes, Jackson's longtime veterinarian. Supposedly, it costs over $75,000 a month to care for the many rescued wildcats at Tippi's cat sanctuary. If you have the money, you can likely take *better* care of wildcats in a large animal sanctuary, where they would have acres and acres to run and roam, while having personal attention from veterinarians to the stars. Likewise, if you're trying to raise a tiger in a tiny Bronx apartment like Antoine Yates did in 2003, don't be surprised when he mauls you. Just don't try to blame it on a pit bull when you go into the ER (thankfully, the ER doctors didn't believe that such a severe wound could be caused by a dog and reported Mr. Yates to the police).

Can I leave my cat out all night?

I recently had a client bring in her cat with severe jaw fractures and head trauma. The owner found her cat with dried blood all over his nose and ears and noticed that he couldn't close his mouth. I suspected that he had been hit by a car, and he was actually quite lucky: he took most of the blunt force injury to his head, not his vital organs. The owner then proceeded to tell me that he stays out all night long, but that she had an outdoor "cat house" for him. She typically let him out when she got back from work (at 5 P.M.), only to let him back in at 5 A.M. when she woke up. Inappropriate, folks! People, these are our loved ones here! Would you like to be left outside for twelve hours without food, water, or shelter? While you may think it's "freedom" for him, you're sacrificing your kitty to the roads, the cars, the stray dogs, werewolves, boogeymen, and everything else creepy that comes out only at night. To top it off, this cat was declawed, so he had no way of truly protecting himself from other animals. Besides, your neighbors probably don't appreciate having their yard being your kitty's overnight litter box (see "Do I have to get rid of my cat when I'm pregnant?" in chapter 9). After a $1,000 lesson and jaw fracture repairs, the owner finally saw the (indoor) light.

So, how do you convert your late-night partying cat to a mellow evening cocktail cat? Here are a few tricks to train your cat to come back in (and stay in!) for the night. When you call your cat back in, feed him his dinner as soon as he walks in the door. That'll motivate him to come to you when you call him in for the night. Try shaking a Pounce treat container so he recognizes the "dinner bell" and runs back home for some feasting. Feeding him before he goes out doesn't help decrease the amount of animals he preys on or birds that he kills, by the way. Once he's in for the night, make sure to provide lots of stimulation for him (see "How do I exercise my fat, indoor cat?" in chapter 5 for more details). You just might be able to convert him to a snuggling nighttime love bug.

Is it safe to let the local stray become our family's new pet?

Before you start feeding that outdoor cat you see in your backyard, check to see if Feral Franny has a collar. If she does, don't feed her. Not only will her owner be wondering why she's getting fatter and fatter, but you don't know if she has a special medical condition (like inflammatory bowel disease, kidney failure, or even diabetes) that precludes her from being fed certain types of cat food. Also, if you leave food out, you'll soon attract all the local cats around, and before you know it, you'll be on the news for having a hundred cats hidden in your house. You'll also become known as the newest free kitty litter box on the block, and all those feral cats will be using your yard as their new toilet. Lastly, Feral Franny will start coming around more and more frequently, and you may now be the proud owner of a new cat, as she'll start depending on you for her food and water.

I'm always paranoid that kindhearted people unknowingly adopt previously owned cats, and while they may think that they're rescuing this feral kitty from the depths of despair, she may already have a good home that has paid to spay or neuter her. If the "feral" cat is neutered and declawed, make sure that you post signs and try looking for her true owner before you steal her away. After all, if someone paid for these surgeries, chances are the cat's not feral and may have a home somewhere. Try posting signs around the neighborhood, advertising on Craigslist.com or in the local paper, or calling the local humane society to be sure her owners aren't searching for her. If there's no luck, then she may be all yours to adopt after all.

If you elect not to adopt this stray and are being a good Samaritan, please bring her to a vet or humane society. There, she can be scanned for a microchip to make sure someone else doesn't own her. If you decide to keep her after all, make sure to take her to a veterinarian right away to ensure that she's healthy. She should also have a simple blood test done for feline leukemia or kitty AIDS (see "What are FIV and FeLV?" in chapter 2). Since you don't know her rabies status, she'll need to be vaccinated also. Before you take her home, get a flea and tick preventative placed on her; after all, you don't want to bring in her new fleas to your nice, plush, carpeted house. Keep her quarantined inside a small bathroom or in the basement (away from other animals) for at least one to two weeks to make sure she doesn't transmit anything to your other housecats. Ideally, keep her indoors only, as she was a street cat and may soon wander off again, after you just paid to "Jiffy Lube" her (see "What's a feral cat?" in this chapter). Hopefully, after you've done all that, she may soon make the perfect addition to your house. Just remind your kids that you can't take every single stray that comes your way. While it's a good deed, you'll soon be overrun with cats. Instead, pawn them off on your friends!

Chapter 8

POISONING
THE PUSSY

AS an emergency specialist, I see the whole gamut of poisonings. One of the most common toxicities I see is rat poison—not the rat per se but the unlucky dog or cat that ate the bait. I *used* to think, geez, how hard is it to hide the poison in an area where your cat can't get to it? Then I learned my hard lesson . . . One day, I brought home some rat poison (I know, I know, but I hate mice in the house with their dirty little feet walking all over my grub). I tucked the green cube of poison deep into the back, dark corner behind the dresser. It was totally cat-proof. Far, far away, right? I walked back into the room twenty minutes later only to find Seamus batting the d-Con around like a toy. Ahh! Yikes! Bad owner, bad owner! Since then, I learned my lesson and decided that poisoning any creature is bad news. So if this vet can't keep poison away from her own pets, what's an owner to do?

When cats do something bad, we owners just chalk it up to their nature; after all, they're curious, right? This chapter will entertain you with all of the bad things a good cat can do, some of which may prompt an emergency visit to the veterinarian. Find out if your house is *really* kitty-proof and what household toxins are deadly to your cat. We all know the hazards of over-the-counter medications and antifreeze, but did you know that the bouquet of flowers your beau just brought home might also kill your more loyal four-legged feline? See if you really pass the cat-proofing test.

What are the top ten toxicities for cats?

And now, the list you've all been waiting for. The annual 2006 list of toxic titans according to the American Society for the Prevention of Cruelty to Animals Animal Poison Control Center.[1] Without further ado, the top ten cat drug overdoses are:

1. Canine permethrin insecticides (flea ointment): Yeah, you read that right. Canine! Read the label before you put that on your cat. Canine does not equal feline!

2. Other topical insecticides (still flea ointment): Getting the hint? Cats are very sensitive to flea control!

3. Venlafaxine: Your cat will be just as depressed as you are once he eats your antidepressant.

4. Glow jewelry and sticks: A mere $800 later, you *were* the light of my life.

5. Lilies: For once, the boyfriend shouldn't have gotten you flowers.

6. Liquid potpourri: Your cat couldn't stand the smell of his litter box either.

7. Nonsteroidal anti-inflammatories (i.e., Advil): Your headache just got a lot worse.

8. Acetaminophen (i.e., Tylenol): Your migraine just got *much* worse.

9. Anticoagulant rodenticides (rat poison): A mouse's revenge.

10. Amphetamines (uppers): No catnap today!

Now that you've seen the list, don't be like the rest of America. Simply (yeah, right) make sure all drugs are well hidden in cat- and kid-proof containers in the bathroom medicine cabinet, keep toxic houseplants out of your house (see "Can household plants be poisonous to cats?" below), read those flea product labels carefully, and don't hide your rat poison under the dresser for your cat to play with (the way this veterinarian once did). Hide these toxins from your kitties, and avoid having to call a pet poison helpline.

Can household plants be poisonous to cats?

While cats are carnivorous, I find that most cats like to chew on the occasional plant. While there's no specific scientific reason for why cats do this, we think it's because they may feel like they need more fiber, that they just want some chewing variety in their life, or because they want to induce vomiting so it's easier to pass that hair ball. Whatever the reason, as an avid plant (and of course, animal) lover, I find that my spider plant or any frond plant takes most of the chewing abuse by my cats. In fact, I have a huge variety of plants in my house, and purposely sacrifice my spider plant so Seamus and Echo leave my other plants alone.

While most household or outdoor plants are only mildly toxic to dogs, some can be extremely poisonous to cats. In general, *most* household plants are relatively safe, but some can cause minor vomiting, drooling, or diarrhea. The most commonly implicated plants are the popular household plant dieffenbachia or those hard-to-kill philodendrons. Ironically, the least toxic plants are the ones that people think about the most. Most people are taught that poinsettias are poisonous but have never heard that other plants like Easter lilies are *more* dangerous. Poinsettias are commonly implicated as a "poisonous plant" but generally only cause clinical signs consistent with licking a cactus (not fun!). Thanks to that irritating, bitter milky sap in the leaf, which contains calcium oxalate crystals, you'll notice Felix instantly drooling, pawing at the outside of his mouth ("Agh! What the heck? This ain't no spider plant!"), and showing signs of oral irritation, gastrointestinal symptoms (like vomiting and diarrhea), lots of drooling, nausea, and hypersalivating. Luckily, your cat instantly realizes this and stops munching.

Please note that there are a few poisonous plants that can cause *serious, fatal, rapid* poisoning, and veterinary care should be sought immediately. Some plants can cause more serious signs like heart arrhythmias (kalanchoe) or even fatal kidney failure. These include Easter, Asiatic, Tiger, Stargazer, and Oriental lilies and even some species of daylilies. With lily ingestion, cats can die within two to three days despite aggressive medical treatment. Eating as little as one Easter lily leaf, petal, or stem will result in signs of fatal, severe, acute kidney failure, such as not urinating, vomiting, lethargy, and general malaise. I always spread the word, especially to outdoor gardeners or around Easter time, as my own sister's cat (which I gave her), Oscar, died of this. My sister's housemate received a bouquet of flowers, and unfortunately Oscar found the one Easter lily in the bouquet and chewed on one or two leaves. It was absolutely heartbreaking. This is a vet's plea! Please make sure to heed caution when bringing in new plants into the house or yard. It's not worth chancing. And while I'm on my soapbox, the next time you talk to a florist, make sure they educate their clients about how poisonous these bouquet flowers can be.

According to the American Society for the Prevention of Cruelty to Animals (ASPCA) Animal Poison Control Center, here are the top ten most common poisonous plants for pets (with their common clinical signs listed):[2]

1. Marijuana (incoordination, seizures, coma, drooling, vomiting, diarrhea)

2. Sago palm (liver failure, vomiting, diarrhea, depression, seizures)

3. Lilies (cats only—acute kidney failure)

4. Tulip/Narcissus (vomiting, diarrhea, drooling, depression, seizures, arrhythmias)

5. Azalea/Rhododendron (vomiting, drooling, diarrhea, weakness, coma)

6. Oleander (vomiting, arrhythmias, hypothermia, death)

7. Castor bean (vomiting, diarrhea, weakness, seizures, coma, death)

8. Cyclamen (vomiting, diarrhea)

9. Kalanchoe (vomiting, diarrhea, arrhythmias)

10. Yew (vomiting, diarrhea, heart failure, coma, trembling)

You can find a list of nontoxic plants for dogs and cats at the ASPCA website (see Resources).

As with all poisons, you should bring Felix to a veterinarian for "decontamination" as soon as you find out that he ate something he should not have. That's a fancy way of saying that we'll induce vomiting, empty his stomach, and then pump it full of activated charcoal to prevent absorption. We can only do this decontamination within the first few minutes to hours of ingestion, as otherwise he may have already absorbed the poison from his intestines. So always bring Felix in as soon as you suspect a poisoning. When in doubt, call a pet poison helpline or poison control just to double-check if you need to rush Felix into the animal ER.

If you can't keep your cats away from your plants, here are a few suggestions. Get rid of all the poisonous ones. Absolutely no lilies in the bouquets or in the house (you can always request that your florist not put any lilies in!). If Felix goes outside, dig up all the lilies in your yard just in case (you can give them away to friends far, far away from your yard). Better yet, supervise Felix while outside and keep him away from anything that isn't clean, fresh, and fertilizer-free. For your indoor plants, move them to a higher shelf that Felix can't reach. Some people use double-sided tape on the furniture or shelves so their cats will avoid the shelf with all the plants on it (see "Why does my cat use my couch as a scratching post and how do I make him stop?" in chapter 2). Once Felix's paws feel the awkward sticky tape, he'll leave that shelf alone (until your housecleaner comes over and wonders what is going on). Another option is to buy or grow some kitty grass (which you can find at a pet store), as Felix may preferentially chew on this instead (which may stave him off your other plants). Otherwise, buy a sacrificial spider plant. Your other plants will appreciate this.

Tigger likes the tinsel on the Christmas tree. Is this OK?

Getting ready to decorate that Christmas tree? Do Tigger a favor and avoid the tinsel. That shiny, stringy tinsel looks like a fun play toy, and knowing how much he likes to chew on plastic bags, rubber bands, and ribbon, tinsel doesn't fall too far behind. You may think it's cute that Tigger's helping you decorate, but in reality all that tinsel can ball up into a tangled knot, get stuck in the stomach and intestines, and result in what we call a *linear foreign body*. What can happen is that part of the tinsel gets wrapped around the base of the tongue, or even stuck in the stomach, while the rest of the string starts slowly passing into the intestines. With the normal contractions of the intestines, the tinsel starts sawing through the tongue, esophagus, stomach, and intestines, resulting in your Christmas bonus going toward Tigger's thousand-dollar surgery. Do yourself a favor and donate the tinsel to a non-cat household!

Why you shouldn't floss your teeth . . . unless you flush.

Just in case you didn't get the previous point, linear foreign bodies are very common in cats (I'm talking to you, bud!). Because cats are inquisitive in nature, your mint dental floss just became a really cool, cheap chew toy . . . so you think. So do what your dentist recommends. Floss. Just carefully dispose of the floss, and either flush it or put it inside a covered garbage can. Don't tempt fate by leaving it precariously placed, dangling over the side of the garbage can for your cat to play with.

If I see string hanging from my cat's butt, should I pull it?

Nothing's worse than having my friends or family call me at 1:36 in the morning to ask me this. While it sounds gross, this does indeed happen. When in doubt, you should leave anything related to your cat's anus up to your veterinarian, as we're (unfortunately) pros at that end of the cat. If something's stuck, let the pros fix it. Do not pull it yourself! Terrible things can happen, like rupturing your cat's intestines or colon.

Cats have a history of eating more than just an inch or two of string (which *should* easily pass if it's that small of an amount), but when they go for one to two *feet* of string just to show you that they can, that string can get stuck at an attachment point, which acts as an anchor. This occurs most commonly at the pylorus (the end of the stomach) or the base of the tongue. If you pull on it, it can plicate the intestines, pulling them all together and even sawing through the thin intestinal lining. Perforating the intestinal wall can result in a severe abdominal infection, and often cats don't survive from this septic peritonitis. Keep all ribbon, string, tinsel, yarn, dental floss, knitting materials, shoelaces, cassette tapes (are you getting the hint?) away from your cat. If you're playing with her favorite feather-on-a-string toy, just make sure you're supervising her the whole time, and then be a good owner—keep it out of her reach during non-playtimes.

If I see string hanging from my cat's mouth, should I pull it?

In case you didn't get the hint from above, leave medical stuff to the pros and do not pull! Your cat's intestines will thank you for not unprofessionally pulling. Trust us—it took us eight years of schooling to figure out how to do it, so leave it to us. If the string is wrapped around the base of your cat's tongue, you could cause severe injury. When in doubt, hold on to a section of the string (without getting bitten or applying any tension) while you frantically find someone to drive you to an emergency clinic right away. And whatever you do, don't cut the string. We need to be able to see it. Just keep it out of the way as much as possible, so your cat doesn't swallow more. You can even carefully tape it to your cat's collar as you frantically find a vet.

Can I give my cat a Tylenol?

Too cheap to take your cat to the veterinarian and want to home-medicate him yourself? Pay attention (especially you, Dr. M.D.)! Over-the-counter medications such as Tylenol, Advil, or naproxen are nonsteroidal anti-inflammatories (NSAIDs), and even one pill can *kill* a cat. Cats are very sensitive to NSAIDs (actually, they're pretty much sensitive to all drugs) because they have an altered liver glutathione enzyme system that prevents them from being able to metabolize certain drugs well. With NSAID toxicity, side effects include severe stomach ulcers, gastrointestinal signs such as vomiting or black, tarry diarrhea (which is caused by digested blood in the intestinal tract), kidney failure, or even seizures or coma. Definitely not fun, and *your* headache will have gotten much worse! Whether you accidentally or intentionally gave your cat an NSAID, bring your cat to a veterinarian right away for emesis induction (pumping his stomach and inducing vomiting), activated charcoal (to bind up the toxin), IV fluids, and antiulcer medication.

If your cat gets into Tylenol, his face will turn puffy and his tongue blue, his liver will be thrown out of whack, and he'll likely need to be treated with oxygen, kitty blood transfusions, and medications to fix the altered oxygen and red blood cells. Your emergency vet bill will be about ten times higher thanks to your self-appointed vet degree. The cheapest emergency bill a client of mine has ever had for a Tylenol poisoning occurred when the owner rushed her cat in after dropping a pill on the floor. She couldn't find the gel capsule and was convinced her cat ate it. For just $150, I examined her cat and "medically" removed the sticky Tylenol pill stuck to her cat's furry belly. If only you could be so lucky . . .

Are all flea products the same?

Many people use permethrin- or pyrethrin-based flea products from pet stores on their dogs. Permethrins are man-made chemicals, while pyrethrins are naturally made and were originally discovered in chrysanthemum flowers. While that makes them sound safe, they aren't—at least not for cats. Cats are very sensitive to the effects of pyrethroids (the general family of chemicals) and are usually exposed accidentally or when Mr. Pet Owner thought, "Well, if it works for small dogs, it must work for big cats!" This toxicity can result in severe muscle tremors (which look like seizures), dehydration, hyperthermia, and death if left untreated. If you notice this, bathe your cat with a safe, gentle liquid dishwashing soap (like Dawn) and then rush him to a vet. If you can't bathe your cat (scratching, hissing, general craziness, and skin-a-flyin'), bring your cat into a vet immediately so we can do it. Luckily, most cats will survive and recover if treated aggressively with supportive care, including intravenous (IV) muscle relaxants (methocarbamol), IV Valium (if seizing), and IV fluids.

Let this be a lesson to you—avoid using dog products on your cat. Remember that a lot of the over-the-counter flea sprays, powders, and collars are often not particularly effective, so stick with prescription-strength, veterinary-recommended products like Advantage, Frontline, or Capstar if your cat is flea infested. These can be purchased from your veterinarian and will cost far less than a two- to four-day emergency stay for the poisoning. Trust me.

If you use the veterinary-recommended stuff as prescribed, and your cat still has a rare reaction, contact a veterinarian immediately. Mild irritation or skin hypersensitivities (Echo lost hair transiently where I applied the ointment) can often be treated by washing off the ointment with Dawn or liquid soap. If the area is still irritated, you can consider opening up a vitamin E capsule and applying the contents there or even applying the gel from your aloe vera plant.

It's 2 A.M. Do I need to bring my cat into the emergency vet?

Ah, cats. We love 'em, but less so at 2 A.M. when they're dry-heaving. What if your cat still continues to vomit multiple times? When do you decide to bring your cat into the ER?

Can you wait to take Felix to your veterinarian in the morning? What's the rush?

When in doubt, call your veterinarian or an emergency clinic for counsel on whether to bring your cat in for an emergency visit. Some sure signs to bring your cat to the ER include difficulty breathing, open-mouth breathing, panting, a respiratory rate over fifty breaths per minute (hint: count the number of breaths in fifteen seconds and multiple by four to get the total breaths per minute), excessive drooling, hiding (under the bed, in the closet), not moving, straining or making multiple trips to the litter box, profuse vomiting, sitting over the water bowl and not moving, seizing or twitching, any kind of trauma, any kind of toxicity, or any string hanging out of any orifice. While this list isn't complete, it's a good initial guideline. When in doubt, please seek veterinary advice immediately. You won't regret playing it too safe with your fuzzy feline.

Why are air fresheners poisonous to cats?

Boyfriend complaining about the kitty litter odor? Thinking about hiding the odiferous essence of your cat with artificial sweetness? Don't worry about your Glade PlugIns, but if you're trying to cover up that litter box smell with liquid potpourri, be careful. The type of potpourri we're talking about is melted or heated over a candle and can often be found in stores like Yankee Candle, Target, and Bath and Body Works. While you may think that cats are smart enough to avoid an open flame, they can't seem to resist that weird-smelling, melting liquid on top of it. This liquid is made up of detergents and essential oils and can be very irritating to the esophagus and mouth. Not only does licking a few laps cause oral ulcers, drooling, nausea, and vomiting, but it can also cause depression, neurologic signs, and low blood pressure.[3] Because it's irritating to the esophagus, you shouldn't induce vomiting at home (nor should your veterinarian); rather, try "dilution is the solution to pollution"—and give your cat some milk or water. Unfortunately, cats aren't smart enough to stop at one lick when it comes to liquid air freshener, so when in doubt, avoid this kind of air freshener in your house. You'll have to find another way of hiding your litter box smell from your loved ones.

Why are glow sticks poisonous?

You know those fun glow-in-the-dark plastic jewelry pieces your kid makes you buy at baseball games, Fourth of July celebrations, or on Halloween? They are safe . . . until your cat, dog, or two-legged pet bites into them. The oily liquid that lights up the plastic is called dibutyl phthalate, and while its toxic, fatal dose is really high (poor lab rats had to eat a lot to *die* from it), Phoebe will notice an immediate effect with just a tiny amount ingested. The massive drooling and instant nausea that come with ingestion usually limit how much Phoebe will lick. Thankfully, it tastes so nasty that Phoebe won't eat enough to kill her or make her belly glow. You can just wipe it away and offer a tasty treat (try Gerber turkey or beef baby food or canned tuna juice) to dilute that nasty flavor stuck in Phoebe's mouth. If you just finished watching *CSI*, are really bored, and want to play with that black light of yours, you can take Phoebe into a dark room to find out where any extra liquid may be lingering. When in doubt, just keep those glow sticks away!

Why can't rat poison kill only rats?

If your cat is too lazy to catch that mouse in your house, be careful putting down d-Con or any anticoagulant rodenticide. That's a fancy way of saying that this specific type of rat poison causes internal bleeding because it is a vitamin K inhibitor (which is normally made in your liver). Believe it or not, this is the best type of poison to buy, as it's reversible and treatable. Other types of rat poison include bromethalin (which causes brain swelling) and cholecalciferol (which causes high calcium and kidney failure), and neither of these has antidotes. Pick your poison carefully. Remember, if this veterinarian can accidentally poison her cat, you can too. Be careful with that stuff!

Chapter 9
SEX, DRUGS, AND ROCK AND ROLL

AH, the juicy chapter. When it comes to cat sexual organs, this species is confusingly backward, so it's no wonder people have so many questions. I once had an owner bring in her intact female cat (in other words, she wasn't spayed) during an insanely busy day in the ER. The poor, exhausted owner was trying to convince me that something was drastically wrong with Frolicking Fanny. Not only was Fanny screaming, stalking her owner, keeping her owner up during the night by crying constantly, and following her from room to room acting really needy, but apparently Fanny was also having severe back spasms. After paying $150 for an ER fee, I had to break it to her that this is what a cat in heat looks like, and that's why we tell owners to get them spayed or neutered before six months of age. When owners have to succumb to the torture of a yowling, overly friendly cat who is trying to get laid, they usually learn their lesson quickly and commit to neutering by six months from then on out.

Bob Barker and veterinarians are always preaching about spaying and neutering, so find out in this chapter if it really helps decrease the risk of cancer. Get a birds-and-bees' view of what you should be ready for when it comes to four-legged cat sex. If your kid asks if Kitty can have one litter, find out what you're about to commit to. If you don't know that female cats are "induced ovulators" and that you may need to use a Q-tip in weird places to help bring your queen into heat, then you may not be brave enough to breed your cat. Find out what a queen in heat looks like, or if she needs to wear sanitary pads when in heat. Find out if there are cat sperm donors out there or where you even go to find an intact tomcat to breed with your cat. How come you never see a cat's penis? Did you know it's barbed and spiked (the penis, not your tomcat's hair)? Read on—and discover what it's all about!

Why is it so difficult to sex a cat?

I'm embarrassed to admit this, but I had a hard time sexing kittens (in other words, determining if it's a female or male cat) even during my first year in vet school. It's an acquired ability. Cats are hard to sex because they don't have that classic penis or prepuce sticking out. Unlike dogs, who have their penis near their belly button, cats have their penis underneath their tail. In fact, their penis is backward and tucked inside unless they're urinating or mating. Sometimes you'll be able to feel two tiny testicles right next to it, but leave this palpating to your veterinarian, or your cat will think you're very, very strange. When you look at your cat's nether region under his or her butt (or the fancier, scientific term "anus"), you'll see a little hole or orifice just below the rectum. If that orifice looks like a small dot, then it's a boy (and no, he won't appreciate you trying to extrude or pull out his penis to double-check). If it's a bigger dash, then it's a girl (so she can fit in the dot, if you know what I mean). Don't feel bad if you can't sex your cat. As I said, even yours truly had a hard time sexing kittens, so don't worry if you try and fail. I've seen lots of Clarences that become Clarissa, or Toms that become Tomi, so when in doubt, have your vet do a double take. Leave the sexing to the professionals, and if even they aren't sure early on, pick a gender-neutral name (or a new vet).

Why do tomcats have bigger heads?

A tomcat is an intact male cat that hasn't been neutered. Tomcats are well known for their "distinctive," malodorous urine and their talented spraying ability. But the trade-off is that they look so cute! Owing to the effects of testosterone, tomcats develop large cheek pads to make them look bigger, larger, and meaner and to protect them while scrapping with another tomcat. Unfortunately, these large, pinchable cheeks get smaller once neutered. Regardless of how cute tomcats are, when in doubt, you don't want too many (i.e., any) tomcats hanging around your house, yard, or garden, as they'll only attract *more* territorial, spraying tomcats—leaving your yard urine soaked and stinking.

Is it true male cats have a backward (spiked) penis; or "Why do alley cats scream?"

Ever wonder why those darn alley cats make so much noise? There's a good reason. The male cat has a backward spiked penis with sharp barbs, so anytime he finds an intact female cat, some screaming occurs. Ouch! Female cats are induced ovulators (i.e., they need lots of vaginal stimulation to release an egg for conception), and male cat penises were evolutionarily designed to scrape the inside vaginal wall to induce ovulation. Shudder. Fibrous barbs cover the length of the penis, which help stimulate the female to ovulate. To top it off, cats are superfecund, which means they can have litters from multiple fathers during multiple (painful) breeding attempts.

So while it's awful to listen to the screaming, you have no idea how painful it really is!

How come I never see my cat's penis?

That's not a bad thing, right? Cats have backward anatomy, and unlike a dog, whose prepuce ends near the belly button, cats have their penis tucked away under their tail. Not only is it pointing the wrong way, but it's got a large bend it in naturally (which allows him to twist and turn to help breed a queen). Cats, apparently, are very private and never show it (unlike your excited dog, who likes to whip out his lipstick (see my other book, *It's a Dog's Life ... but It's Your Carpet*).

If you do see your cat's penis sticking out, something is very, very wrong, and you should seek veterinary attention immediately. A normal cat will tuck that bad boy away. In fact, if veterinarians need to place a urinary catheter into the penis, we have to sedate male cats, as they don't appreciate us "straightening their bend." If your cat's penis is sticking out, it usually indicates that he has a urinary obstruction. In other words, something may be lodged in the tip of his penis (like a stone, crystal clump, or plug of mucus), preventing him from being able to urinate (see "Why do cats lick down there?" in chapter 2). He may be straining and unable to urinate, and if you're observant enough to catch this, rush him to a veterinarian. We won't think you're dirty for looking down there.

Why does my cat spray?

Nothing's worse than when you walk into your friend's house and it reeks of cat pee, right? I guess having your *own* house reek of cat pee would be worse. Regardless, how does one go about telling your host? Being a veterinarian, I can have this awkward conversation easily, since I can use my "medical expertise" and kindly say, "Dude, what's wrong with your cats? It smells like piss down here!" Of course, that's when your friend starts whipping out the black light and showing you all the cat piss sprayed on the walls, complaining how his wife's cats are destroying his basement, and what ever should he do? Then your friend starts inviting you over more and more to help with their kitty litter problem. In exchange for dinner and beer, I have to hound them to buy another litter box, show them how to scoop their nasty, overflowing litter box more often (instead of dumping the whole bin every ten days), yell at them for not putting enough clumping kitty litter in the box, and set up the extra litter box for them. Is it worth the dinner invite? Sure . . . I'll work for food (or beer . . .).

Cats spray or mark by typically backing their rump to a vertical object, quivering their tail, and releasing that nasty concentrated urine all over your newly painted walls and your carpet. It's their way of leaving their business or calling card and telling other cats around them that this is their property. While this is typical for tomcats roaming the neighborhood, we can occasionally see neutered cats doing it (usually males, although the occasional spayed female will mark also). Indoor neutered or spayed cats typically will mark for behavioral reasons: if there is interhousehold cat aggression, poor litter box husbandry (your litter box is too disgustingly dirty, and your husband has slacked on litter box duty!), not having enough litter boxes, or exposure to other cats.

If your cat is spraying in your house, try a few hints. First, use a black light to identify where the stink is, and add more litter boxes to the area where he's spraying. Try taping some plastic over the area where the spray is and having it run into a litter box; that way, it protects your walls and encourages your cat to use the litter box instead. Clean your litter boxes more frequently (see chapter 3 on kitty litter care), and make sure to use clumping litter. Finally, if your cat is ogling cats outside on his turf, block his view so he can't see them. If your cat sees outdoor cats through the window, or if you're bringing home cat scent, your astute cat may start spraying if he thinks another cat is going to encroach upon his territory—he doesn't want to have to share you with anyone else. Prevent neighborhood cats from coming into your yard by talking to your neighbors (plead for the great indoors), using a Super Soaker, or using a motion-activated device to scare them away. Consult with an animal behaviorist, and consider drug therapy if all else fails. Feliway, an over-the-counter feline pheromone, has been shown to help decrease the incidence of spraying (see "What's Feliway and what does one do with these feline pheromones?" in chapter 5). If all else fails, sounds like Prozac may be in your cat's future.

Are there cat sperm donors out there?

There are cat sperm donors and sperm banks out there, but they're usually designed to help preserve the genetic variety in endangered, not household, cats. The Zoological Society of London set up a big cat–sperm bank a few years ago to help preserve future generations of rare, endangered wildcats such as the Amur tiger, the Sumatran tiger, and the Amur leopard (of which there are only about thirty left in the world). If they didn't do that, there would be a lot of inbreeding of the remaining few captured zoo wildcats out there. Also, with recent advances, artificial insemination (AI) is more efficient, allowing multiple cats to be bred with just one "donation" (as there are millions and millions of sperm, and it only takes one).

In our domesticated cats, sperm donors and AI are pretty rare, as most breeders just use a stud cat (one lucky tomcat that gets to breed as his job). Thanks to the advent of the Internet, it's so much easier to find contacts through breeding forums where you can "borrow" (i.e., pay for) a stud cat. While dog breeders use AI more frequently, we don't find the same in cat breeders—guess their toms have more fun that way!

What does a cat in heat look like?

Once you notice your first, official heat cycle as a cat owner, you'll run to go get your cat spayed. *Estrus*, or heat, is when your cat's hormones are raging, and it's basically the best time for your cat to get pregnant. Typically, this occurs around nine to ten months of age but can occur as early as four months of age, especially when there are long sunlight hours. Cats can cycle every two to three weeks, for a few days at a time, torturing you until you spay, breed, or Q-tip your cat (see "What's this about a Q-tip?" in this chapter). She'll display all the provocative, sexy traits to try to entice a male. You'll notice your cat's suddenly becoming much friendlier, rubbing her head, back, and body all over your legs as she chases and follows you around the house. She'll start meowing like you've never heard her call before and may even start spraying urine to attract some manly tomcats. Don't worry—it'll end in a few days, and by then your Ambien may have worn off anyway.

Just so you know, we veterinarians don't do routine in-heat cat spays in the ER just because Frolicking Fanny is keeping you up. Do the earth a favor and spay her early, so she doesn't contribute to pet overpopulation and so you can sleep. If you're thinking about breeding her, ask yourself if this twice-monthly ritual for months on end is worth it. Or you can always invest in a good pair of earplugs . . .

What's this about a Q-tip?

While researching this book, I was aghast to find out what was circulating out there on the Internet. Did you know you can find out how to calm down your cat while she's in heat? While the easier, veterinary-advocated way is to get her spayed, you can indeed soothe your kitty during her heat cycle. There are detailed (too detailed, if you ask me) ways on how to stimulate your cat's vagina with a Q-tip so she'll stop hollering and crying for some loving. Because cats are induced ovulators, your cat won't release an egg until she's physically stimulated (which is one of the reason why there are barbs on a tomcat's penis). Once stimulated, her heat cycle will quickly end. Without stimulation, her heat cycle will *eventually* end after a few torturous days (with howling, attempts to escape to find some loving, and constant attention-seeking behavior), only to restart a few weeks later. I won't put the details of the Q-tip here, but you can indeed find out all the information that your heart desires, in as much graphic detail as you want, thanks to Google.

Is a "spay" the same as a "hysterectomy"?

We veterinarians hear it all. Let me clarify a few things for you, as all this terminology can be confusing, especially since vets don't always use the same terms as human doctors. You are either bringing in Lizzie for the noun, an ovariohysterec-tomy (OVH), or for the verb, the action of being spayed; you are not, however, bringing her in to be hit over the head with a spade. I often hear, "I think she's already spaded." *Really*.

In the United States we commonly perform an OVH, where we remove both the ovaries and almost the entire uterus, leaving just the remnant cervix behind. A hysterectomy is when just the uterus is removed, leaving both ovaries within the abdomen. While this will prevent any unwanted preg-nancy, Lizzie is still exposed to the hormonal effects of both estrogen and progesterone, which are produced from the ovaries that were left inside. These hormones result in in-creased risks of mammary gland (breast) cancer, so we gen-erally don't recommend this. Another rarer option is to just remove the ovaries (leaving the uterus in the body); this is an ovariectomy and is rarely, if ever, done in veterinary medicine. There won't be any hormones released once the ovaries are removed, but you might as well take out the plumbing while you're in there.

Is "neutering" the same as "castrating"?

Neutering means to "desex an animal."[1] Although technically it can be used with both females and males, for some reason, the term "neuter" has been more commonly associated with males. Apparently, the word "castration" causes men to an-thropomorphize, running frantically out of the veterinary hospital with their cat and leaving more intact cats out there in the world. Regardless of which term you use, neutering or castrating basically leave the penis, penile urethra, and scro-tum intact and unharmed but remove both of the testicles from the scrotum.

Cat neuters are different from Fido's neuter. In Max, your cat, we make a small incision right on top of the scrotum and gently remove both testicles, while leaving the scrotum and penis intact (don't worry—that sac will heal and shrivel up). When we neuter Fido, your dog, we make a small incision just in *front* of the scrotum and remove the testicles through this incision (pushing them up from the scrotum). Dogs don't seem to heal well from having their scrotum scalpel-ized, so it's done slightly differently. Regardless, you, Max, and Fido will barely notice it even happened after a few days.

The benefit of neutering Max is that his nasty man-habits (like spraying concentrated, foul urine all over your walls) will slowly diminish over the next few days to weeks, but so will those cute, large, pinchable cheeks. The good news is that Max will be less aggressive, masturbate less, and mark his urine less frequently, and you'll help decrease pet over-population at the same time. Unfortunately, his metabolism will slow down in the process, so make sure to cut back on the amount you're feeding him once he recovers from his neuter.

Do cats masturbate?

Yes, cats do masturbate or "dry hump," as we veterinarians jokingly call it. When you notice your cat biting onto a blanket, kneading with his front limbs ("making muffins"), and doing the humpty dance, I'm afraid you've just walked in on your cat masturbating. This looks quite different from regular wool sucking or making muffins (see "Why does my cat suck on my cashmere sweater?" in chapter 3 and "What's my cat doing when he's kneading my blanket?" in chapter 4), as you'll notice a happier grin and more hip motion involved with the "dry hump." Thankfully, your neutered cat shouldn't produce anything, so don't worry, Grandma's antique quilt will stay clean. Even neutered cats do this occasionally, so don't be alarmed—it's all just part of nature!

What's a cat sex change?

You may hear this term used out there, but we veterinarians don't usually call it this (as it's not really accurate). In veterinary medicine, we don't usually do a true penis amputation. Sometimes a perineal urethrostomy (known as a "p.u.") needs to be performed if your cat has a history of having multiple urinary obstructions (see "Why do cats lick down there?" in chapter 2). While this isn't a penis amputation or sex change per se, it does open up the diameter of the urethra (the tube from the bladder to the penis tip) so that your cat can pee out stones and crystals and such. Boy George will still be a boy, don't worry.

Does neutering cats decrease the risk of cancer?

When in doubt, neuter your cat sooner rather than later. A recent study[2] by Overley and colleagues proved that cats spayed prior to six months had a 91 percent reduction in the risk of breast cancer compared to intact females. This study also found that having multiple litters didn't decrease the cancer risk either, as it does in humans. That said, get your cat spayed before a year of age to minimize cancer risk *and* pet overpopulation. Veterinarians harp on spaying and neutering your cat because it reduces your cat's overall cancer risk; while female dogs may have a fifty-fifty shot of having benign versus malignant lumps in their breasts, mammary masses in cats are highly associated (90 percent) with *malignancy*—in other words, it's a really aggressive type of breast cancer in cats. If you're rubbing your cat's belly and feel lumps near those nonfunctional nipples, bring in your kitty to a vet right away to make sure it's not breast cancer.

Male cats rarely develop prostate cancer or prostate problems. First of all, they have a very tiny, vestigial prostate compared with men's or dogs', so it doesn't cause them as many problems as it does for their human and canine counterparts. Second, we veterinarians don't see a lot of well-cared-for male intact tomcats (as they are usually running the streets feral), so we see a skewed population. In other words, there may be a lot of prostate cancer out there in those cats, but we never see them because male tomcats have a shortened life span because of their rough life on the streets and their infrequent visits to the veterinarian. Thankfully, prostate or testicular cancer is quite rare in cats. That said, even the rare male cat can get breast cancer, so when in doubt, get that lump checked out.

I want my cat to have one litter to teach my child about the miracle of life. What do I need to know?

Want to recoup some of the money that you paid for that purebred Persian or teach your kids about the miracle of life? Rent a video. While you may think it's fun to let your cat have one litter, raising a litter is financially, emotionally, and physically a lot of work. One routine litter could potentially cost the following:

- Veterinary exam of the mother (to make sure she is healthy, well vaccinated, FeLV- and FIV-negative, blood typed, dewormed, and doesn't have a heart murmur or any other congenital/inherited diseases that you do not ethically want to breed and pass on)

- Potential male stud breeding costs

- The first set of vaccines and deworming for the whole litter

- Milk replacer and kitten food

- Sleep, because you have to wake up every one to two hours to bottle-feed the kittens for the first two to three weeks if the mother cat rejects them

- A clean, warm, isolated nursing area

- Heating lamp and pad

- Veterinary emergency visits in the rare event the mother needs a Cesarean section (averaging $2,000)

- Advertising to sell the kittens or time to find homes for all of them

Seeing the miracle of life firsthand is not as priceless as you think. More important, remember that millions of animals are euthanized a year because homes can't be found for them. Please consider all this when breeding your queen. "Don't breed or buy when homeless animals die!"[3] If you still want to experience the miracle of life, you have a few animal-friendly options. Consider fostering a pregnant cat from a local humane society or rescue group. These organizations are constantly looking for foster parents to help provide a more natural "home" environment when these four-legged moms are close to delivering. You may be able to witness the delivery at home, although more often people miss the delivery. Because cats are private and don't want to put on a show, you may go out for a movie and come home to six kittens. Thankfully, your household of children won't be disappointed if they missed the "show," as they'll be excited just to see the newbies!

Are there inbred big cats?

Hopefully, outdoor feral, intact cats aren't too common of a problem in your neighborhood, but remember that one tomcat can produce lots and lots of offspring—he just cares about breeding and passing on his genes, not the consequences of inbreeding. If his progeny are the only intact, feral cats around, guess who he's going to "play" with? Likely, his daughter or even his mother (gross!). This contributes to more and more cats being inbred.

This happens in big cats too, and unfortunately, owing to certain species being endangered, more and more inbreeding is occurring, as there are fewer mates to mate with (and you thought you had it bad with the dating pool out there). A decade ago, the Florida panther was near extinction, making the genetic breeding pool smaller and smaller. As a result, inbreeding occurred, and heart defects, overall poor kitten survival, and low sperm counts were abounding in panthers. A controversial breeding plan was implemented, and while there were naysayers about the use of human intervention, the genetic breeding pool was increased by adding in a few nearby Texas panthers. These hybrids (mixes of the two) were found to have a higher survival rate with fewer defects and helped increase the number of panthers by increasing the genetic breeding pool.

Is it true a lot of zoo cats have kitty AIDS?

Many viruses can affect different families of cats, regardless of how big or small they may be. Viruses such as feline panleukopenia, feline leukemia, feline infectious peritonitis, or even feline immunodeficiency virus (FIV) are not only seen in our housecats but also in wildcats such as lions. Even canine distemper (despite its canine name) can affect these wildcats! Chances are most of the lions you see in the zoo are infected with FIV (which is the cat equivalent of human HIV) and likely caught it the same way our domesticated cats did—by blood or saliva exchange. While we may see a shortened life span, weakened disease resistance, chronic gum disease, and weight loss in our housecats with FIV, many lions seem to carry the disease without being clinically affected. That said, don't worry—you can't spread it or get it from your cat or your local lion at the zoo.

Can I get herpes from my cat?

Did your veterinarian just diagnose your new kitten with herpesvirus? Before you freak out or blame your boyfriend, know that feline herpes isn't contagious to you—just to your other cats. Chances are your cat probably caught it at the shelter from another sneezing cat. Feline herpesvirus is in the same family as that virus that gives you those nagging cold sores on your lip. In cats, herpes is one of many viruses that contribute to upper respiratory infections (often called URIs, for those of us too lazy to spell the whole thing out) and results in symptoms like sneezing, a snotty nose, or runny eyes. In severe cases, herpesvirus can lead to ulcers of the eyes and mouth too.

Just took a trip to the groomer? Returning from the shelter? Coming home from the veterinary clinic? Too many cats in the household? These things are all very stressful to our four-legged felines, and they'll show you by sneezing snot everywhere. With stress, the virus recrudesces, which means symptoms show up when you and your cat are too stressed to deal with it. Because it's a virus, it doesn't usually need to be treated with antibiotics unless your kitty's snot just turned green, which means there's a secondary bacterial infection too. Unfortunately, herpes can spread to your other housecats, and before you know it, your whole house—yourself included—won't be able to deal with the stress!

Unfortunately, there's no cure for this virus, so symptomatic supportive care is necessary. Make sure to do things like wiping away Noso's eye and nose discharge, keeping his nostrils clear of all those caked-on goobers, and ensuring he's eating tasty treats. Because cats won't eat food they can't smell, sometimes microwaving canned food for a few seconds to warm up the pungent, liver-flavored goodness is all you need to get Noso eating. Lastly, you can even take Noso into the bathroom with you when you shower; mind you, don't put him *in* the shower with you—just bring him in the bathroom. That humidified, hot steam will help clear up his schnoz also. If all those tricks of the trade don't work, consult with your veterinarian about antiviral medications, lysine (an amino acid that helps with URIs), or even some antibiotics if absolutely necessary.

Why do cats like to have their rump smacked?

Both female and male cats enjoy having their rump smacked, even if they're neutered. You may notice your cat arching his back, lifting his tail high in the air, and wanting more. Is it because your cat is kinky or into neutered S&M? While we know that female cats in heat really dig this (it's their way of showing off their parts and enticing the male), I've noticed both sexes enjoy rump smacks. What's probably happening is that your cat can't rub or scratch that lower part of his back despite his dexterity, and those smacks give that area some much needed lovin' and touchin'.

Are kittens identical or fraternal twins?

Even though your new batch of rescued shelter kittens all look alike, they are unlikely to be identical twins and are more likely to be fraternal twins. Identical twins occur when one fertilized egg (from one sperm) splits into two (or more) embryos, resulting in the same genetic makeup for each kitten (sort of like Mother Nature's own clone). Kittens from the same litter likely formed from individual eggs and sperm. In fact, if the queen bred with multiple tomcats (bad girl), she could have kittens from multiple sires all within the same litter. Thankfully, she doesn't differentiate and loves them all equally. Only DNA testing would reveal which father fathered whom, and I doubt your cats want to travel all the way to Montel or Jerry Springer to find out more.

Do I have to get rid of my cat when I'm pregnant?

No! Despite what your M.D. may tell you, you don't have to get rid of your cat just because you are pregnant. Cats are carriers of the infectious single-cell parasitic organism *Toxoplasma* but are rarely affected by it—they just shed it. Nearly a third of adults in the United States have antibodies to *Toxoplasma*, which means they have been exposed to this parasite but don't have an active infection from it. The three main ways to become affected by or exposed to *Toxoplasma* include (a) transmission from a pregnant mother to her unborn child when the mother is infected during pregnancy (pretty rare), (b) handling or ingesting undercooked or raw meat from infected animals (like venison, lamb, or pork), or (c) inhalation or ingestion of the oocyst (an early "egg" stage of the *Toxoplasma*)[4] by soil or litter contact (from your cat's litter box or when gardening or playing in your kid's sandbox). This last way is particularly high if you live in a region where outdoor cats may be burying their stool in your garden or your kid's sandbox—yet another reason I'm an advocate for indoor housecats.

People at risk for toxoplasmosis are pregnant women and immunosuppressed individuals (the elderly, the young, those with lupus or AIDS, or those undergoing chemotherapy). Unfortunately, symptoms include miscarriage, mental retardation, deafness, blindness, and rarely, death. Pregnant women should be blood tested for *Toxoplasma gondii* before becoming pregnant (or during pregnancy), because if they are already seropositive (in other words, positive on a blood test), they are *not* at risk of acquiring a primary, acute infection during pregnancy. For once, testing positive is actually a good thing! This means that she's already protected, and is armed with antibodies in her immune system to fight it off. A woman is more at risk if her test comes back negative, as that means she doesn't have any previous exposure (or protective antibodies) to *Toxoplasma*. Because she's negative, she absolutely shouldn't get any exposure during pregnancy.

Toxoplasma oocysts take more than twenty-four hours to "ripen" and become infectious to you, so daily cleaning of the litter box helps avoid this problem. Knowing this, if you are pregnant, it is safer for you to clean the litter box once or twice a day for the duration of your pregnancy, or better yet, let your partner have litter box duty for the next nine months. It's for everyone's safety. Surprisingly, some veterinarians or cat owners may not even be seropositive, despite living with cats for decades, and this may be due to lack of exposure, an unexposed cat, or neurotically clean litter box habits.

Instead of getting rid of your cat, an easy, simple way to protect yourself from *Toxoplasma* is to make sure that you wash your hands thoroughly with soap and water after handling litter, soil, sand, compost, or meat. In addition, make sure to wash your garden vegetables thoroughly with water before eating them, and boil all water from unknown water sources (i.e., when you're camping). Cooking meat at 152°F (66°C) or higher will kill *Toxoplasma*. Keep your cat indoors, as they first are exposed to toxoplasmosis while hunting vermin. Also, cover children's sandboxes when not in use to discourage cats from defecating in them (they do look like one big kitty litter box, if you must know). In general, consult with both your veterinarian and doctor about possible zoonotic (infectious between animals and humans) diseases that can occur. There are also many online references available for more great information on what precautions you should take.[5] (See Resources.)

Will my cat and my baby get along?

Depending on your cat, his desire for attention, and his level of jealousy, I always caution pet owners to carefully acclimate their cats to the newborn human. I've heard lots of success stories, and I've watched my nephew get along fine with his housecat, Elliot. In fact, I'm amazed at how well Elliot has adjusted to the two-legged tot, allowing the child to climb all over him, pull his fur, and sit on him at times. God bless 'em, those four- (OK, and I guess those two-) legged creatures!

There are many things you can do during your pregnancy (and before you bring home your newborn) to help your cat adjust to the weird smells that will come out of that two-legged kid of yours. Start by leaving some of the toys and strollers that you will be using around the house. Turn on the (annoying) music of the playpen so your cat gets used to the new noises. Play a baby video with sounds of a child crying to help prepare him for the noisy wails that will soon constantly bombard the house (lucky you!). It's also a good idea to bring home a blanket with your infant's smell from the hospital before you bring your kid home. Let your cat sniff and investigate this new smell. Most important, make sure to show him the same level of attention, even when your newborn is around, so your cat won't get jealous or feel blown off. Hopefully, your cat will learn to positively associate calm and happiness with the baby smells and the newborn.

On a side note, do make sure to baby-proof and cat-proof your house carefully. Baby pacifiers, food-encrusted baby bibs, and toys can easily be chewed and get stuck in your cat's intestines. When your toddler starts walking, there's a good chance he or she will want to chase the kitty. Try not to leave your cat alone with your newborn or young toddler unsupervised. Chances are your cat will run away, but if your toddler starts running, too, your cat has a harder chance for escape. Because of this, I recommend having a kid-proof room. Provide your cat with a room that is baby gated so your kitty can escape the tail pulling and "nice touches." That innocent tail or ear pulling could result in a bad scratch or bite, so you want to be there to defuse any situations that might occur.

Chapter 10
THE VET AND
THE PET

WHILE this book may not answer all your veterinary questions, hopefully it'll help you find the qualities that you're looking for in a vet for your pet. This chapter will address some honest questions that you've been wanting to know but are often too embarrassed to ask your veterinarian. Find out why cats don't get Lyme disease and why heartworm disease is becoming more prominent in cats. Discover what the side effects from vaccines are and how often you should *really* get your cat vaccinated. Likewise, find out if you just keep your cat indoors, if you even ever have to take her to a vet again. (Yes, you do.)

For those of you well-balanced multispecies pet owners, I already provided a lot of this information in *It's a Dog's Life . . . but It's Your Carpet*. Nevertheless, this stuff is so important that I wanted to make sure all my feline-loving friends also have this information. Want to know what it takes to become a veterinarian? Is it true that it is harder to get into veterinary school than it is medical school? Today, over 70 percent of graduates are women.[1] Why? Find out the differences between your medical doctor, your veterinarian, and your veterinary specialist. This chapter will take you behind the scenes of the seven to thirteen years of veterinary training it took for your veterinarian to tell you if your cat farts, why your cat attacks you when you pet his belly, or if it's OK to declaw your cat. Most important, find out what your veterinarian wants *you* to know about being a smart consumer and pet owner. Discover how to find the best veterinarian for you and your family and what questions to ask to ensure that your four-legged furry feline is in the best possible hands! Remember, veterinarians want you to be a well-educated consumer for your cat, and by empowering yourself with knowledge, you can work with your veterinarian to best promote your kitty's health. It's not every day a veterinarian gives you honest advice about your cat and his or her health—you can't afford not to listen!

My cat gets really stressed from the vet trip—can I just keep him indoors and never vaccinate him again?

If your cat gets really stressed from car trips to the veterinarian, it doesn't mean that you should bypass routine veterinary care. Believe it or not, it's important to make sure you bring in your cat for an annual exam. Your veterinarian may be able to detect medical problems much sooner than you think just based on historical information that you provide them (such as weight loss and excessive drinking or urinating) and the clinical and physical examination findings (like feeling for small kidneys or a thyroid nodule). This is especially important as your cat turns middle-aged (eight to nine years of age) or approaches those geriatric years (fourteen plus!), where kidney failure, hyperthyroidism, diabetes, inflammatory bowel disease, and cancer are more prevalent. Also, if your cat gets *that* stressed out from going to the vet, call your vet in advance and ask for some feline floaters (such as acepromazine or Torbugesic) to mellow him out so the whole trip is smoother for everyone involved (you, your vet, and your cat!).

While annual vet exams can slowly become expensive, you can work with your veterinarian to find a vaccine protocol that best suits you and your cat, so you're not paying for it year after year if those vaccines aren't necessary. Because of the side effects (albeit rare) from vaccines, I work individually with clients to find out their cat's exposure to other animals and the owners' financial means, to figure out what works best for them and their cat. In general, once your kitten has gone through a full kitten series and annual vaccines for several years, I recommend an annual *exam* but vaccines every two to three years, depending on your cat's exposure (see "How many vaccines does my cat *really* need?" below). When in doubt, find a veterinarian who supports you in this decision—if not, find another vet!

How many vaccines does my cat *really* need?

In general, if your cat is indoor only and doesn't have exposure to other cats, he or she should have gone through a full kitten series (one vaccine every three to four weeks from six weeks of age until sixteen weeks of age) and then an annual feline distemper and rabies vaccine for three to five more years. After that, your cat should have an *annual* exam, but vaccines could be reduced to every two to three years, depending on your state's law for rabies. If your cat is exposed to the great outdoors, or if you are fostering or rescuing lots of cats, your cat should potentially have annual vaccines in addition to the feline leukemia (FeLV) vaccine. Because the FeLV vaccine isn't as effective as the feline distemper vaccine (see "Should I get my cat vaccinated for feline leukemia?" below), consult your veterinarian about whether or not your cat really needs this, and if the risks outweigh the benefits. If your cat doesn't have exposure to Lyme disease, giardia, or FeLV, I don't think it's necessary to give your cat extra vaccines. Utilize appropriate guidelines such as the American Association of Feline Practitioners Feline Vaccine Advisory Panel Report (which can be found at the AAFP site as well as veterinary sources such as the Cornell Feline Health Center on the Internet) to help you and your veterinarian work together to establish an appropriate protocol for your cat.[2]

Should I get my cat vaccinated for feline leukemia?

While the feline leukemia (FeLV) vaccine offers *some* protection, it isn't 100 percent effective. While it decreases the *severity* of the disease process, it doesn't *prevent* the deadly virus. This is very different from the feline distemper vaccine, which is almost 99 percent effective and *prevents* the disease. The FeLV vaccine is one of the least effective vaccines marketed, and because of rare risks associated with the use of this specific vaccine (specifically, a skin cancer called fibrosarcoma), we currently *only* recommend it for high-risk cats: those that romp around outdoors, are immunosuppressed, or have exposure to a lot of random cats (in other words, if you're fostering lots of cats and exposing them to your own!). More information can be found at a great website for both veterinarians and owners at Cornell's Feline Health Center (see Resources).

Why shouldn't my cat get vaccines between the shoulder blades?

In 1991 veterinarians started noticing that cats were developing connective tissue tumors (sarcomas or fibrosarcomas) in similar areas to where they were getting vaccinated. Since then, there has been an association with certain vaccines and sarcoma development. As scary as that sounds, know that veterinarians are looking out for the health of your cat, and it's important to realize that cats still need certain vaccines to prevent fatal diseases. While the risks of developing a sarcoma from a vaccine are very, very minute, your veterinarian should work with you and evaluate your cat's risks for diseases, making sure not to overvaccinate.

There are also scientific guidelines to help evaluate which specific diseases and vaccines your cat needs. The Vaccine-Associated Feline Sarcoma Task Force, which has veterinary representatives from organizations such as the American Veterinary Medical Association, the American Animal Hospital Association, the American Association of Feline Practitioners, and the Veterinary Cancer Society, has recommendations and guidelines that are available to your veterinarian.

Current recommendations are to administer certain vaccines in specific areas of your cat's body. Because fibrosarcoma is so invasive, we want the vaccine to be given as far down on the leg as possible; that way, in the rare chance that a sarcoma develops, we can remove as much as possible (by potentially amputating the affected limb) or we can irradiate the lower limb (with radiation therapy) rather than the whole body. For this reason, we no longer give vaccines between the shoulder blades. Currently, we veterinarians are taught this little key: right rear = rabies, right forelimb = feline distemper, and left hind limb = feline leukemia. Seems like a lot to know, but that way you have the insider's scoop on where you'd like your cat to be vaccinated.

Should I get my new kitten tested for FeLV or FIV?

I'm always amazed that people don't know if their cat has ever been tested for feline leukemia (FeLV) or kitty AIDS (feline immunodeficiency virus, or FIV). In the ER, people classically reply to my query with "Well, I'm not sure, but he's up to date and vaccinated for it, I think." People—you need to know this! As mentioned earlier, the FeLV vaccine is very ineffective, and most vets don't vaccinate for it. Know your cat's status when it comes to these two important diseases. After all, don't you make sure your new beau is HIV-negative before letting him into your bed? To save yourself a lot of future grief, do yourself (and your other housecats) a favor and blood-test any cat before you even *think* about adopting him or her. Some shelters test all cats automatically—but don't assume that, and *always* double-check this test at your own veterinarian. The FeLV blood test is really easy to run and usually automatically comes with the FIV test too. This test only requires a few drops of blood, and for those of us with obsessive-compulsive disorder or attention deficit disorder, we can get the test results back within minutes before bringing Tigger home. If you keep your cat indoors, you usually need to have this done only once or twice within the first year of his life, unless other medical problems arise.

If your cat does test positive for either virus, consider consulting an oncologist or internal medicine specialist to see what other treatment options are available. Unfortunately, Typhoid Tigger's life span will be dramatically shortened because of these diseases. My philosophy is that we can still provide him the best quality of life before he gets really sick, as each happy, good day gained is icing on the cake, right?

Most important, remember to keep Typhoid Tigger away from your other housecats and indoors only, as he should have minimal exposure to other cats. That's how infectious these viruses are to other cats! After all, you don't want your cat spreading anything fatal throughout the neighborhood, do you? Your front yard would be t.p.'d (and justifiably so) for life!

Why don't cats get Lyme disease?

Cats seem to be pretty resistant to spirochete infections (which are those nasty spiral organisms that cause diseases like Lyme or leptospirosis). Research studies have shown that while cats can get experimentally induced Lyme disease, it's pretty rare.[3] Maybe it's because cats are such fastidious cleaners that the ticks don't have time to attach for long enough. Ticks need to typically stay attached for forty-eight hours before Lyme disease is even transmitted, and by that time your cat may have chewed off the tick, eaten it, and spat it back out. While we let our cats out into our backyards, they don't usually go hiking through the woods, so they may just have less exposure to ticks than our canine companions. Lastly, we may not see Lyme disease as commonly in exclusively outdoor cats just because they don't have the same ability to be monitored as closely as indoor cats. Those farm cats that are out wandering the tick-infested woods may not have owners that notice any symptoms, or these owners may not bring in their farm cats for routine exams, making feline Lyme disease underrepresented and underdiagnosed.

What is cat scratch fever?

John Travolta didn't invent it, but Ted Nugent wrote about it.
Cat scratch disease (CSD), or cat scratch fever, is caused by

a bacterium called *Bartonella henselae*. Approximately 40 percent of cats carry it during some stage of their life, although it's more commonly found in kittens. Although cats are carriers, they aren't symptomatic from it (Do you notice a trend here? Cats like to carry diseases but have so many lives, they aren't affected by them!), so it's nearly impossible to know which cat could potentially spread it to you. An inadvertent scratch can result in general malaise (what we vets fondly call ADR, or "ain't doin' right"), fever, swollen lymph nodes, poor appetite, and back pain in *you*.

While it's easily treatable, CSD can lead to severe symptoms, particularly in people who are immunosuppressed (from organ transplants, cancer therapy, or from HIV/AIDS). Although this doesn't mean you should be scared of your cat, you should take certain precautions. Don't let your kitten or cat scratch you. (Duh!) Rough play with a kitten should never be advocated, as it can result in a scratch and teach an impressionable young one that roughhousing and scratching are OK. Also, make sure to keep your cat's nails short. If you are scratched, use soap and running water to scrub the wound extensively, and consult with a medical doctor immediately.

Because *Bartonella* can be found in fleas, it's also important to use appropriate flea control—not a cheap flea collar, but the real stuff (see "Are all flea products the same?" in chapter 8). It's unlikely you'll get it from a flea bite; otherwise they'd call it flea bite fever, right? Nevertheless, you want to prevent a flea from transmitting this bacterium to your cat. If you do get scratched and you start noticing symptoms, contact your physician immediately and tell him or her that you were scratched by your cat. And no, you can't take your cat's strawberry-flavored Clavamox instead of going to your medical doctor.

Plague: The new rage . . .

Hard to believe, but plague is back, and you and your cat may be susceptible. If you live in the Rocky Mountain area or near the four corner states, pay close attention. The *Oropsylla montana,* or rodent flea, can be a vector for plague, which is caused by the *Yersinia pestis* bacteria. If this flea bites an infected rodent, the flea can spread plague, which can be lethal and highly contagious, even with treatment. So why are cats to blame? Well, cats are really susceptible to plague if they are outside roaming around, catching infected rodents (and bringing them home to you). They can get infested with fleas and spread the disease around. Yet another reason to keep your cat inside, right?

While there is treatment for plague, it should be identified and treated quickly with appropriate antibiotics (like tetracyclines). In the past three decades, fifteen instances of cat-associated human cases were seen. We veterinarians care about this disease a lot because 50 percent of people who got plague were veterinarians! Yikes! Makes you not want to hug or kiss your vet. All joking aside, this is a very serious disease and needs to be legally reported to the Centers for Disease Control and Prevention, which then reports it to the World Health Organization. Unfortunately, plague is also a possible chemical warfare agent. Seriously. Anyone want to buy some Advantage flea preventative?

Why is heartworm disease becoming more prominent in cats?

If you own a dog, you know how important (yet expensive) it is to have your dog on heartworm preventative (that tasty once-a-month chewable pill). For you non–dog owners, heartworm is a tiny but destructive little worm (or microfilaria) that is transmitted by mosquitoes into your four-legged friend's bloodstream. These microscopic worms lodge in the pulmonary vessels and the heart of your pet and cause severe, potentially life-threatening complications. If you live in a mosquito-infested area (like the Midwest, East Coast, South . . . get the point?), then both your dog and outdoor cat may be at risk. In dogs, clinical signs of heartworm disease include coughing, exercise intolerance (tiring out easily), weight loss, fainting, and fluid in the belly (which are signs of right-sided heart failure), while in cats the disease is more subtle but just as deadly. In cats, heartworm disease can cause difficulty breathing and chronic vomiting, and contrary to dogs, there's no good "cure."

Luckily, protection from heartworm disease is easy—your cat only needs to take a pill once a month to kill off any microfilaria before they grow into adult worms. I didn't start my indoor cats on this until I moved to Minnesota. I've found persistent mosquitoes inside my house despite all that I do (even in the winter). Because there's no cure in cats (only preventative medicine), I'd rather treat my cats than risk them getting the disease. So, no, it's not a hoax by your veterinarian to get more money. In fact, diagnosing heartworm disease in cats is more expensive than preventative pills (as you need special blood tests and lung fluid washes). So, if you live in Minnesota, the tristate area, or anywhere mosquitoes love to bite, and you own an outdoor cat, do your cat and yourself a favor, and talk to your veterinarian about a once-a-month preventative pill.

What is your vet really doing when she takes your cat into the back room?

It's always awkward to get manhandled (or in this case, cat-wrangled) in front of owners, because both owners and cats don't understand what we're doing when we're restraining them (the cat, that is, hopefully not the owners). Because it's painful to see your cat manhandled (even with the best intentions), and because some cats are actually worse in front of their owners than without them, we often take your cat into the dreaded "back room" so we can appropriately restrain your cat on his or her side while we gently draw some blood. Unlike your human phlebotomist who can tell you to stop squirming, we don't have that luxury for cats, so oftentimes we have to use a "party hat" (i.e., muzzle) or even a towel (i.e., the burrito) to restrain them. The sooner it's done, the sooner it's over, so please trust us—it would just stress you out more to see your cat in a kitty blanket burrito.

How often do vets get bitten by cats?

As my veterinary school anesthesiologist Dr. John Ludders used to teach us, "Better living through chemicals" or "Just say yes to drugs." Only the scientific kind, folks, not the recreational kind. I bring this up only because veterinarians would get bitten a lot less if we all used more drugs.

At my last visit with my medical doctor, she asked me if I felt like I was in a safe, nonviolent relationship while looking at my arms and hands. Apparently, my arms looked like they had been hit with a razor (although my job in the ER is hard, it's not *that* bad), thanks to clawing and biting cats. Unfortunately, getting scratched and bitten (along with being pooped, peed, vomited, and anal sac'd on) just comes with the territory. Because cats don't understand why we are trying to restrain them (we promise, it's only to help them!), they often fight back with their claws and teeth as the good Lord intended them to. For you declawers out there: your cat is more likely to *bite* us now that their claws are gone. We actually prefer scratchers to biters. While it looks more traumatic to have long rakes of flesh ripped off your arms, it's less likely to get infected. Cat mouths are nasty, and bite wounds easily get infected. Thankfully, I'm averaging a bad cat bite (requiring IV antibiotics and a human ER visit) once a decade (knock on wood).

Since my last serious cat bite, I have practiced veterinary medicine in ways that are smarter and less stressful; in other words, I practice what Dr. Ludders preached: chemical restraint. I utilize my technicians to do all the restraining, use sedation to make it less stressful for the schizoids (only available for your cat, not *you!*), and practice my ninja skills in the mirror every night so I have quicker reflexes. Of course, if you want to help me out, there are oral sedatives that you can give your kitty an hour or two before you bring him into the vet clinic; I guarantee that you, your veterinarian, the technical staff, and your groovin' calico cat will appreciate it! Call us before you come, and we'll happily dole out some sedatives for your cat's next visit. It'll save me a lot more skin.

Are veterinarians allergic to cats?

Surprisingly, a lot of veterinarians I know are indeed allergic to cats, but despite the itchy, red eyes and sniffling, we battle through it. It's hard to give up one's love for kitties just for some minor suffering, right? Thanks to Claritin (and even more thanks to over-the-counter Claritin), allergic veterinarians are now able to keep their jobs without the constant postnasal drip. Don't take it personally when we choose not to snuggle your kitty right up to our faces, as sometimes it makes us have a flare-up. If you see your vet's puffy red eyes and notice that she is crying, don't take offense: she's either severely allergic to your cat or she's just been dumped.

Do vets have fleas?

Ever wonder why your veterinarian wears scrubs instead of nice clothes to work? We don't do it because our clothing budget ran dry, or to look smarter or cooler—we do it to prevent us from carrying infectious diseases back home to our *own* pets. We change out of our scrubs at the end of the day, as we don't want to carry home any fleas, feces, anal sac juice, blood, vomit, urine, or infectious viruses. Which is not to say that our after-exam apparel doesn't pick up that musky animal aroma, which is why I shy from Thomas Pink shirts and jump straight into street clothes. On my twenty-fourth birthday, my mother kindly told me that if I wore less flannel and fleece, I'd have been able to find a man by now (she's very well intentioned, I promise!). When she tries to buy me nice clothes, I can actually get away with a kid's favorite excuse: "But I'll just get crap on them!"

Veterinarians are lucky that the risk of infectious diseases from cats is lower than it is in humans—I don't have to worry as much about getting a needle prick or spilling cat blood into my many cat scratches, as there are fewer diseases that cats can give to humans. However, there are still some that can be transmitted by contact or random bodily fluids, such as ringworm, parasites, mites, fleas, and other fun afflictions. And so, yes, unfortunately, despite all preventative measures, we veterinarians occasionally bring home the rare bug or flea. Occupational hazard, my friend. Now you see why by disinfecting one's stethoscope, or having multiple sets of scrubs to change in to, we can avoid a lot of these infectious problems. In general, you'll be glad to know that veterinarians are pretty clean people. Despite being covered in bodily fluids, we are careful about not carrying anything home. Don't be scared to be near us (unless we don't like you!)

What are the top ten reasons people bring their cats to the vet?

According to Veterinary Pet Insurance, the top ten reasons people bring their cats to the veterinarian are:

1. Urinary tract infections
2. Upset stomach
3. Kidney failure
4. Skin allergies
5. Diabetes
6. Respiratory infections
7. Ear infections
8. Tooth extractions
9. Colitis (diarrhea)
10. Hyperthyroidism

Of course, this list is skewed to general practice, and what I see in the ER is a bit scarier and a whole lot sicker. Kidney failure, cancer, jaundice, anemia, upset stomach, urinary or urethral obstructions, heart failure . . . the list goes on.

What's a veterinary specialist?

To become a veterinarian, one must take a science-dominant premed course load (including anatomy, physiology, organic chemistry, biochemistry, and physics) during undergraduate studies. I was an animal sciences major at Virginia Tech and spent a lot of my classes on farms and in laboratories. Some veterinary schools allow you to apply as a sophomore or junior in undergraduate school, so you can enter veterinary school one to two years early (saving you $20,000 to $50,000 per year, potentially). Once in veterinary school, you undergo a rigorous four-year graduate-level training in all the -ologies (pharmacology, physiology, toxicology—sound fun?), with your last year acting as your clinical year (where you play doctor under the guidance of faculty) in the hospital. Upon finishing veterinary school, you are a full-fledged veterinarian and can practice as a veterinary general practitioner.

As of December 2007, there were 58,240 veterinarians in the United States in private clinical practice including small animal (dogs and cats), exotic (birds, wildlife, and zoo animals), large animal (cattle, sheep, and other weird assortments like emu, alpacas, elk, llamas, and so on), equine, porcine, and other random assortments.[4] An additional 29,000 are in public or corporate employment including research, government, and academic fields. In total, there are 83,730 veterinarians in the United States, with approximately 8,885 specialists.

A veterinary specialist is someone who has gone on to do even more advanced or secondary training through a rigorous one-year internship, followed by further training in a residency, which is an additional two to four years; hence, all those extra letters behind their name (i.e., DACVECC). There are currently multiple specialties, such as veterinary anesthesiology, behavior, cardiology, dentistry, dermatology, emergency and critical care, internal medicine, neurology, nutrition, ophthalmology, oncology, pathology, radiology, surgery, and zoo medicine.

Currently, the trend is for veterinary medicine to become more progressive and specialized like human medicine. In general, veterinary specialists see referral cases that may be more complicated. For example, if your cat requires advanced chemotherapy or an ultrasound of his heart, he may need to see a board-certified veterinary specialist in oncology or cardiology, respectively. If your cat has advanced kidney failure, a consultation with an internal medicine specialist is imperative. If your cat needs twenty-four-hour care and is critically ill, he or she may need to be evaluated by an emergency critical care specialist. More information on specialists can be found at the website of the American Veterinary Medical Association (see Resources) or at the specific specialties' websites. My specialty is emergency and critical care, and I am a diplomate of the American College of Veterinary Emergency and Critical Care (DACVECC).

What is Justine's biggest veterinary pet peeve?

On the first day of orientation at Cornell University's College of Veterinary Medicine, the dean of the veterinary college gave us this sage advice: if you learn one thing from veterinary school, learn how to pronounce "veterinarian." It's not "vet-re-narian." It's "vet-er-in-ar-ian." In the same way, it's not "vet-ran," rather, it is "vet-er-an." Could be an Ivy League ivory tower (i.e., snotty) thing to say at our first day at orientation, but it's since become a big sticking point, just as my mad old professor predicted. By now, it's too late—you've already bought the book, and you hopefully won't think I'm too much of a snoot.

Should I trust a veterinarian who doesn't own cats?

Would you trust a chef who won't eat his own food?

I'm going to be controversial here and say that you shouldn't. You don't want to take your kid to a pediatrician who doesn't like kids, right? I'll admit, I'm more of a dog person because I love to hike and get muddy with my pooch, but when it comes down to it, I still adore and love cats. Thankfully, most veterinarians love both, but when in doubt, make sure your vet loves cats as much as you do! I feel that they can empathize more with you and your cat if they actually know what Felix and you are going through. Don't get me wrong—there are wonderful veterinarians out there who may not own cats. Nevertheless, I can pretty much guarantee you that your furry feline won't get the same TLC from a vet who doesn't catnap with one.

Do you do CPR on cats?

Cardiopulmonary cerebral resuscitation, now called CPCR, is indeed performed on animals. Interestingly enough, pigs are actually used for human CPCR research to help improve the outcome and see what drugs work best. We veterinarians evaluate this research and make decisions on how to approach CPCR in the veterinary field. Unfortunately, CPCR is not like what you see on TV shows such as *ER* or *Grey's Anatomy*. We're not giving cats mouth-to-mouth, but we do stick a tube into Felix's trachea to breathe for him. We prefer cat cooties to human cooties any day.

With CPCR, the likelihood of getting an animal back once it has respiratory or cardiac arrested is much lower in veterinary versus human medicine, averaging only about 4 to 10 percent in dogs and cats.[5] It's higher with cats than dogs, and that's probably because cats have nine lives (seriously). Humans go into cardiac arrest from heart attacks and can "more easily" be defibrillated to stop the arrhythmia, but cats rarely get heart attacks, so their cardiac arrests are usually from kidney failure, liver disease, cancer, or other underlying, advanced end-stage problems. As such, once a cat's heart arrests, it's unlikely that veterinarians will be able to revive Felix and even more unlikely that it won't happen again. Make sure to discuss this big decision with your family before it comes to this point in your cat's life.

How much does it cost to euthanize?

Unfortunately, there's a cost to everything, and I've been disheartened to hear clients say "If I knew it was going to be so expensive, I would have just let him die at home!" The price to euthanize Tigger depends on each veterinarian's fees, which can range from $45 to $250, so call around if you are concerned. In general, your family veterinarian or farm veterinarian will be less expensive than going to a veterinary school, although autopsies may be offered at a lower cost there or even be free, since it's a teaching hospital. Regardless, please don't try anything at home. At the same time, some people expect Tigger to "die peacefully at home," when realistically that rarely happens. Don't wait for Tigger to slowly suffer when you could have potentially alleviated any suffering or pain. There are house call veterinarians who can come out to your home so you have more privacy and peace. But either way, you're going to be reaching for the wallet. Just consider it your last gift to your poor, loyal feline friend. And in those last few days, make sure to give Tigger all the tuna and milk he wants!

Do I have to be present for my cat's euthanasia?

The decision to humanely euthanize is very personal, and no veterinarian should *ever* question your decision on whether or not you want to be present for the actual euthanasia. This tough decision is a heartbreaking and emotionally difficult experience, no matter how peaceful we veterinarians try to make it. I always tell owners that their last memory with their cat should be a pleasant one, and if it's the memory of snuggling on the sofa with your kitty or watching him sleep in a sunbeam, rather than watching him pass away in a sterile veterinary clinic, that's OK. If you choose not to stay with your cat, your veterinarian and technician will be with him the whole time, cuddling, holding, and soothing him with an affectionate farewell.

If you do decide that you want to be present during your cat's euthanasia, know that he may show certain signs of relaxation from the sedative and euthanasia solution. I always warn owners that their cat may urinate, defecate, take one last deep breath, or keep his eyes open the whole time, even after he's passed away. Very rarely, some animals may have muscle twitching after they have passed, owing to the calcium and electrolytes in their muscles. Despite describing all that, trust us in knowing that the process is very fast (within a few seconds) but very peaceful. The decision to end suffering or a life is a serious one, but your veterinarian will compassionately guide you through to the end and respect you whether or not you choose to stay.

Can I have a living will for my cat?

When I rescued Echo, I knew he was going to die a potentially terrible death owing to his congenital heart murmur. He'd either have a paralyzing stroke to his back legs (saddle thrombus) or develop fluid in his lungs (congestive heart failure) and have difficulty breathing. In fact, he had orders to be adopted only by a veterinarian, as we veterinarians would know how short his life would be and would be "less attached" that way (yeah, right!). Of course, I fell madly in love with him, but I knew when I adopted Echo that I could grant him a great quality of life (albeit short!) until the time came to humanely euthanize him.

Because I didn't want Echo to suffer, I created a living will for him. I have a detailed list of resuscitation orders for him, so my pet-sitters will know what to do in the extreme condition that they can't get in touch with me during an emergency. I actually have this information saved in the electronic medical record of my pets at the veterinary hospital and often advise other people to do the same. Ask your veterinarian if he offers a living will for your cat, so he'll know exactly what you want done in case of an emergency. Sounds corny (or neurotic) to some (while scaring my pet-sitter in the process), but I think living wills are important for two-legged and four-legged creatures alike. It's not a topic we typically talk about with our loved ones, but by the time we do, it's often too late.

During my residency, I saw all the crazy things that people subjected their pets to, regardless of what their veterinarians recommended. Having put some animals through more than I would have done for myself or my own pets (and seeing them suffer in the process), I decided to get a living will for myself too. I didn't want those same heroics performed on me—I'd rather go peacefully, without being a financial, emotional, or physical drain on my loved ones. It was about the same time when I decided to make a living will for JP, Seamus, and Echo. We all love our pets, and our "love" for them extends in different ways. Just make sure your veterinarian, family, and pet-sitter know your pets have a living will too so they can also respect your wishes.

Do vets do autopsies on pets?

Yes, as gross and scary as it sounds, we vets do autopsies on our four-legged friends. In human medicine, a lowly 10 percent of autopsy[6] rights are granted to hospitals (in other words, most people decline the option to have an autopsy done on their loved one). Likewise in veterinary medicine, the decision to have an autopsy performed may be based on several factors. First, doing an autopsy may affect your wishes for what you do with Tigger's body. Cosmetic autopsies can be performed if you elect to take Tigger's body back for burial or for the pet equivalent of an "open casket," but do realize that if you request a full autopsy, you cannot take Tigger's body back home, unless it is in the form of ashes via a private cremation. This is to protect you so you don't look in the bin to find the organs and tissues. If you elect to have the hospital dispose of Tigger's body medically, you can still get an autopsy performed. The question is, why would you want to?

Autopsies are often of benefit for several reasons. First, an autopsy provides important diagnostic and therapeutic information to your vet—in other words, it may tell your veterinarian if the treatment was working or what the cause for the demise of the patient was. Second, these procedures let us know if there was more we could have done, and autopsies help researchers down the line in being able to more rapidly identify the disease or hopefully find a cure. For the family, autopsies are extremely beneficial if there was risk of something infectious, such as a disease that was contagious to you or your other pets (like feline infectious peritonitis, feline leukemia in the bone marrow, or the rare plague). Sometimes autopsies will help identify causes for sudden, unexpected deaths of our pets, although sudden blood clots (such as a pulmonary thromboembolism or heart attacks) will often not show up in an autopsy. Lastly, autopsies may be needed as part of legal evidence in cases of toxicity or poisoning. If you're worried your neighbor poisoned your cat with antifreeze (which, thankfully, is rare), an autopsy should definitely be performed. Some shelter veterinarians may also recommend doing autopsies if they are concerned about underlying animal abuse, which in many states they are required to report.

Next, your decision to authorize an autopsy on Tigger may be affected by price. The cost for autopsies varies and may be dependent on whether your own veterinarian performs the procedure or whether you have a board-certified pathologist (of the American College of Veterinary Pathologists) perform it (where extensive histopathology, or cell analysis, toxicity screening, or specific diagnostic cultures or tests may be performed). Ultimately, it's the most accurate way of finding out what was going on, when the answer may have eluded all other tests. Once the results of the autopsy are back, it often helps give peace of mind to owners when they find out that Tigger had cancer and that they made the right decision to humanely euthanize him.

What are my options for disposing of my cat's remains?

No veterinarian should ever judge you for the decision you make with your cat's body. If they do, go elsewhere! Some people elect to take their cat's body home to bury in the backyard; just check with your county's laws on this before doing it. Others prefer to have their veterinarian medically dispose of the body, where it is cremated or buried out of sight of the thankful, grieving owners. Other owners elect to have their cat's ashes back. Is this weird or gross? Not at all! To each his own. If keeping your cat's ashes on your mantel is a comforting way for you to remember her, then that's what we recommend. At the same time, some people elect to scatter the ashes in their cat's favorite spots—under her favorite tree or in the garden.

More recent options include having the ashes blown into glass jewelry (see Resources). While this sounds weird to some, I've seen some pieces and they are both artistic and beautiful. While not all of us may want to wear our cat's remains around our neck, artistic jewelry is a clean, safe option—but not without a hefty cost!

Is it true vet school is harder to get into than medical school?

Because there are only twenty-seven (and growing...) veterinary schools in the United States (versus the 120-plus medical schools), getting into veterinary school may be more competitive owing to fewer veterinary school opportunities. On the other hand, maybe it's because of the power, fame, and higher salary of being a medical doctor that more people are seeking that M.D. degree than the D.V.M. degree (or the V.M.D., no thanks to the University of Pennsylvania's love for Latin). Not that I'm complaining—it keeps my job secure! Also, many veterinary schools are state funded, so applicants may be state restricted as to what schools they can enroll in. For example, the Virginia-Maryland veterinary school only accepts a handful of out-of-state applicants a year. So, yeah, I guess it is pretty difficult to get into vet school but not because of more rigorous performance requirements. Veterinary training lasts nearly as long as that for medical school; hence, fewer people may apply to veterinary school owing to the time investment up front and the discrepancy in salary (if this isn't clear, vets make much less than medical doctors). Lastly, as pre-veterinary courses are identical to those for pre-medicine, many pre-vet students end up transitioning to the dark side before their training is through. So if your own doctor ever pats you on the head after giving you an exam, now you know why!

Veterinarians need a minimum of an undergraduate degree (typically three to five years) and four years of veterinary school. The last (fourth) year of veterinary school is the clinical year, where one "plays doctor" by spending time on the hospital floor in various rotations, under the supervision of faculty. After completion of veterinary school, one can go out immediately and practice veterinary medicine as a general practitioner. However, a smaller proportion (approximately 10 to 20 percent) of each graduating class may continue on to advanced specialty training. Often this is followed by a one-year internship in medicine and surgery, and then by a two- to four-year residency for further specialization. So, while every little seven-year-old girl's dream is to be a veterinarian, when she realizes this means at least seven (and up to thirteen!) years of homework and hysterics, she might not stick around. Only those who are truly dedicated see it through, and that's what keeps our profession competitive.

Why are so many veterinarians women?

Prior to the 1970s, veterinary medicine was a 90 percent male-dominant career. This is not too surprising, as it still felt a bit like a 90 percent male-dominated world. It was extremely difficult to get into veterinary school as a female back then. Since then, veterinary medicine has become progressively, incredibly, indubitably more female friendly, as more opportunities for women have opened up. Personally, I think a lot of horse-crazy, stuffed-animal-crazy girls grow up wanting to be veterinarians (until they find out how many years of school it is or that they may have to euthanize animals), so it doesn't surprise me that the field has seen such an influx. While this gender change hasn't been seen in the human medical field, it's still reasonable to hypothesize that the reason there are more women is because we are naturally more compassionate and nurturing and have an innate passion for helping animals. At least, as a woman, that's what I'd like to think.

Do vets hate it when they hear, "I used to want to be a vet, but I couldn't deal with euthanizing animals"?

Yes. Surprisingly, this is not the reason why we wanted to become vets either. Seriously.

Do you see animal abuse cases?

I'm afraid we do, and it's one of the most heartbreaking hazards of the job. Unfortunately, like children, dogs and cats can't pick their owners and some get a bum deal. What's interesting is that you can't always guess or identify who the animal-abusing owner will be. I've had cases where people look completely "normal" and continually pay thousands of dollars fixing fractures, ruptured spleens, internal bleeding, or broken bones. It doesn't take long before the red flags go up.

Animal abuse cases are complicated. Depending on what state you live in, it may be mandatory for veterinarians to report it to the state. Other states are deregulated. Some cases of animal abuse stem from domestic violence, and veterinarians become concerned about the possible repercussions, such as retaliative violence from reporting the case. Abuse-like symptoms could also be due to Munchausen syndrome by proxy, a psychological disease in which the owner hurts their pet to draw more attention to themselves and to feel like a nurturer. I don't know about you, but having my pinkies broken in the name of love, à la Stephen King's *Misery*, doesn't sound like fun. I'm sure the pets would agree, but unfortunately they cannot speak for themselves. Regardless, animal abuse cases are always complicated in nature, as they could hurt more than just the pet.

If you suspect animal abuse, there are places where you can turn. Animal shelters have established animal welfare systems, and oftentimes an animal control officer will investigate the situation. While they may be overwhelmed with numerous cases, know that you have someplace to turn to report a case of suspected animal abuse or cruelty.

How do I know if I've found a good veterinary hospital?

Finding a health care provider that you trust and believe in is imperative whether you are a two-legged or a four-legged client. Things to keep in mind when finding a veterinary practice include the following:[7]

- Do you feel comfortable with the doctor and technical staff? Do they take the time to answer your questions?

- Does the veterinary clinic maintain an organized health record that details prescriptions, physical examination findings, and blood work? Do they give you copies of the blood work?

- Are the office hours convenient to you?

- What payment plans or methods are available?

- What range of medical services do they provide? Do they do in-house blood work and x-rays? Do they have anesthetic machines, oxygen, a full pharmacy, and options for referral if necessary?

- How are emergency calls handled?

- Do they provide nonmedical services such as grooming, nail clipping, and boarding, and if not, can they refer you to such a place?

- Are the veterinarians members of a professional association (such as the American Veterinary Medical Association) or a state veterinary association?

Ask your friends, breeder, or colleagues who their veterinarian is, and shop around. Be a smart consumer for your four-legged feline family member. It's not like you're shopping for a new brand of cat food here; it takes research and forethought to make the best choice. Most important, find a veterinarian who you feel is caring, compassionate, and knowledgeable, explaining all your choices (from medical options to referral to a specialist), and working with you to do what's best for Kitty and for you.

We want cat owners to be smart, fun loving, and responsible. The first step to being a good consumer is to find a veterinarian whom you like and feel comfortable with. Just like with your own health care provider, you should trust and like your veterinarian. If not, seek a second opinion. At the same time, remember what your options are. There is a lot of knowledge available on the Internet nowadays, but you must be able to separate the wheat from the chaff. There is a lot of inaccurate information out there, and your kitty and I would hate for you to make a hasty decision. When in doubt, talk to your veterinarian and remember that you always have the option to seek a second opinion or a referral to a specialist with or without your veterinarian's approval. Become educated on the health of your cat, either by consulting reliable veterinary-based sources or by asking your veterinarian.

Next, maintain an anal-retentive, well-organized medical record for your cat at home, so you have all that information readily available in case of an emergency. One helpful hint: when your cat has blood work done, ask for a copy for your own record. While all those abbreviations and numbers may not mean anything to you, they'll provide a lot of important information to your emergency vet or next caretaker. Finally, make sure your veterinarian has all your up-to-date contact information, including a cell phone number or e-mail address, along with living directives (a living will), if indicated. Be your pet's advocate, because besides you, me, and your cat, no one else can look out for your nonspeaking four-legged friend!

What are the health benefits of having a cat?

Not sure if all that hair-shedding, 3 A.M. vomiting, kitty litter box duty, midnight romps around your head, and kitty litter–dusted bedsheets are worth it? Well, did you know that having a cat can significantly decrease your blood pressure within just a short amount of pet-ownin' time—particularly if you're prone to hypertension?[8] The National Institute of Health Technology Assessment Workshop showed that pets help decrease the incidence of heart disease in their owners. Apparently, non–pet owners are crazier, as having a loyal companion gives people "greater psychological stability," minimizing the risk of heart disease. In addition, people who owned pets were found to make fewer doctor visits for non-serious medical conditions. I'm surprised more health insurance companies aren't giving away pets to keep their costs down.

We cat owners all know that our feline friends are great for stress relief. After a long stressful day at work, it's much easier to unwind and enjoy life when you have a glass of red wine in one hand and a purring cat in the other. We should all learn an important life lesson from our cats—take lots of catnaps, don't stress out, rule the roost, let someone else take care of you and pick up your crap, and be content with the simple things in life—a nap, a sunbeam, and a warm lap to love.

NOTES

CHAPTER 1

1. Leslie A. Lyons. "Why Do Cats Purr?" January 27, 2003, accessed at www.sciam.com/article.cfm?id=why-do-cats-purr.

2. R. Gunter. "The Absolute Threshold for Vision in the Cat." *Journal of Physiology* 114 (1995): 8–15.

3. Paul E. Miller. "Vision in Animals—What Do Dogs and Cats See?" Proceedings, The Twenty-fifth Annual Waltham/OSU Symposium, October 2001.

4. American Veterinary Dental College Position Statement: Feline Odontoclastic Resorption Lesions, accessed at www.avdc.org/FORL.pdf.

5. D. Vnuk, B. Pirkic, D. Maticic, et al. "Feline High-Rise Syndrome: 119 Cases (1998–2001)." *Journal of Feline Medicine and Surgery* 6, no. 5 (2004): 305–312. F. Collard, J. P. Genevois, C. Decosnes-Junot, et al. "Feline High-Rise Syndrome: A Retrospective Study on 42 Cases." *Journal of Veterinary Emergency Critical Care* 15, no. 1 (2005): S15–S17. Amy Kapatkin and D. T. Matthiesen. "Feline High-Rise Syndrome." *Compendium on Continuing Education for the Practicing Veterinarian* 13, no. 9 (1991): 1389–1397.

6. Ibid.

7. L. N. Trut. "Early Canid Domestication: The Farm-Fox Experiment." *American Scientist* 87 (1999): 160–169.

8. www.patentstorm.us/patents/5443036.html.

9. www.freepatentsonline.com/crazy.html.

10. www.lib.unc.edu/ncc/gallery/twins.html.

CHAPTER 2

1. IDEXX Senior Care brochure, accessed at: www.idexx.com/animalhealth/education/diagnosticedge/200509.pdf.

2. B. M. Kuehn. "Animal Hoarding: A Public Health Problem Veterinarians Can Take a Lead Role in Solving." *Journal of American Veterinary Medical Association* 221, no. 8 (2002): 1087–1089. G. J. Patronek. "Hoarding of Animals: An Under-recognized Public Health Problem in a Difficult-to-Study Population." *Public Health Reports* 114, no. 1 (1999): 81–87.

3. Ibid.

4. "Your Cat: Indoors or Out?," accessed at www.hsus.org/pets/pet_care/our_pets_for_life_program/cat_behavior_tip_sheets/your_cat_indoors_or_out.html.

5. Richard D. Kealy, D. F. Lawler, J. M. Ballam, et al. "Effects of Diet Restriction on Life Span and Age-Related Changes in Dogs." *Journal of the American Veterinary Medical Association* 220, no. 9 (2002): 1315–1320.

6. Ibid.

7. A. J. German. "The Growing Problem of Obesity in Dogs and Cats." *Journal of Nutrition* 136 (2006): 1940S–1946S.

8. www.partnersah.vet.cornell.edu/pet/fhc/pill_or_capsule.

9. www.authorsden.com/visit/viewshortstory.asp?id=10278.

10. www.lifestylepets.com/hypocat.html.

11. Steve Sternberg. "To Head Off Allergies, Expose Your Kids to Pets and Dirt Early, Really." *USA Today*, March 19, 2006, accessed at www.usatoday.com/news/health/2006-03-19-allergies-cover_x.htm. Gina Greene. "Kids' Best Friends: Pets Help Prevent Allergies." CNN.com Health. August 28, 2002, accessed at www.archives.cnn.com/2002/HEALTH/parenting/08/27/kid.pet.allergies. D. R. Ownby, C. C. Johnson, and E. L. Peterson. "Exposure to Dogs and Cats in the First Year of Life and Risk of Allergic Sensitization at 6 to 7 Years of Age." *Journal of the American Medical Association* 288 (2002): 963–972. T. A. E. Platts-Mills. "Paradoxical Effect of Domestic Animals on Asthma and Allergic Sensitization." *Journal of the American Medical Association* 288 (2002): 1012–1014.

12. G. M. Strain. "Hereditary Deafness in Dogs and Cats: Causes, Prevalence, and Current Research." Proceedings, Tufts' Canine and Feline Breeding and Genetics Conference, October 2003.

13. G. M. Strain. "Deafness in Dogs and Cats," accessed at www.lsu.edu/deafness/deaf.htm. D. R. Bergsma and K. S. Brown. "White Fur, Blue Eyes, and Deafness in the Domestic Cat." *Journal of Heredity* 62, no. 3 (1971): 171–185. I. W. S. Mair. "Hereditary Deaf-

ness in the White Cat." *Acta Otolaryngologica.* Suppl. no. 314, (1973): 1–48. I. W. S. Mair. "Hereditary Deafness in the Dalmatian Dog." *European Archives of Otorhinolaryngology* 212, no. 1 (1976): 1–14. G. M. Strain. "Aetiology, Prevalence, and Diagnosis of Deafness in Dogs and Cats." *British Veterinary Journal* 152, no. 1 (1996): 17–36. G. M. Strain. "Congenital Deafness and Its Recognition." *Veterinary Clinics of North America: Small Animal Practice* 29, no. 4 (1999): 895–907. G. M. Strain. "Deafness Prevalence and Pigmentation and Gender Associations in Dog Breeds at Risk." *Veterinary Journal* 167, no. 1 (2004): 23–32.

14. D. A. Gunn-Moore and C. M. Shenoy. "Oral Glucosamine and the Management of Feline Idiopathic Cystitis." *Journal of Feline Medicine and Surgery* 6, no. 4 (2004): 219–225.

CHAPTER 3

1. www.peteducation.com/article.cfm?cls=1&cat=1838&articleid=1542.

2. Jacqueline C. Neilson. "Top Ten Behavioral Tips for Cats." Proceedings, Western Veterinary Conference, February 2003.

3. Sarah Hartwell. "The Domestication of the Cat." Cat Resource Archive, accessed at www.messybeast.com/cathistory.htm.

4. J. A. Baldwin. "Notes and Speculations on the Domestication of the Cat in Egypt." *Anthropos* 70 (1975): 428–448.

5. www.karawynn.net/mishacat/toilet.html and www.petplace.com/cats/how-to-toilet-train-your-cat/page1.aspx.

6. www.thecatsite.com/Snips/107/Cat-Litter-The-Dust-Settles.html.

7. Amanda Yarnell. "Kitty Litter: Clay, Silica, and Plant-Derived Alternatives Compete to Keep Your Cat's Box Clean." *Science & Technology* 82, no. 17 (2004): 26.

8. www.minerals.usgs.gov/ds/2005/140/claysbentonite-use.pdf.

9. www.catgenie.com/compare-save/3-save-environment.

CHAPTER 4

1. Karen Overall. *Clinical Behavioral Medicine for Small Animals* (St. Louis: Mosby, 1997).

2. Sharon A. Center, T. H. Elston, P. H. Rowland, et al. "Fulminant Hepatic Failure Associated with Oral Administration of Diazepam in 11 Cats." *Journal of American Veterinary Medical Association*

209, no. 3 (1996): 618–625. Dez Hughes, R. E. Moreau, L. L. Overall, et al. "Acute Hepatic Necrosis and Liver Failure Associated with Benzodiazepine Therapy in Six Cats, 1986–1995." *Journal of Veterinary Emergency Critical Care* 61, no. 1 (1996): 13–20.

3. PetPlace Staff. "Do Dogs Mourn: Canine Grief," accessed at www.petplace.com/dogs/do-dogs-mourn/page1.aspx and Nashville Pet Finders. "Do Dogs Mourn?" ASPCA Mourning Project at www.nashvillepetfinders.com/mourn.cfm.

4. Ibid.

5. S. M. Reppert, R. J. Coleman, H. W. Heath, et al. "Circadian Properties of Vasopressin and Melatonin Rhythms in Cat Cerebrospinal Fluid." *American Journal of Physiology—Endocrinology and Metabolism* 243, no. 6 (1982): E489–E498.

6. David M. Dosa. "A Day in the Life of Oscar the Cat." *New England Journal of Medicine* 357 (2007): 328–329.

7. E. Fuller Torrey and Robert H. Yolken. "*Toxoplasma gondii* and Schizophrenia." *Emerging Infectious Diseases* 9, no. 11 (2003): 1375–1380.

8. Alan S. Brown, Catherine A. Schaefer, Charles P. Quesenberry Jr., et al. "Maternal Exposure to Toxoplasmosis and Risk of Schizophrenia in Adult Offspring." *American Journal of Psychiatry* 162, no. 4 (2005): 767–773.

9. Ibid.

10. Beth Thompson. "Flawed Conclusion Fingers Cats as Cause of Mental Illness." *Compendium on Continuing Education for the Practicing Veterinarian* 27, no. 9 (2005): 648–649.

11. Ibid.

CHAPTER 6

1. Pet Connection Staff. "Pet-food Recall: The Scope of the Tragedy." Universal Press Syndicate, accessed at www.petconnection.com/recall.

2. Ibid.

3. Ibid.

4. Ibid.

5. Ibid.

6. A. J. German. "The Growing Problem of Obesity in Dogs and Cats." *Journal of Nutrition* 136 (2006): 1940S–1946S.

7. D. R. Strombeck. *Home-Prepared Dog & Cat Diets: The Healthful Alternative* (Ames: Iowa State Press, 1999).

8. Charlotte H. Edinboro, Catharine Scott-Moncrieff, Evan Janovitz, et al. "Epidemiologic Study of Relationships Between Consumption of Commercial Canned Food and Risk of Hyperthyroidism in Cats." *Journal of the American Veterinary Medical Association* 224, no. 6 (2004): 879–886.

9. C. B. Chastain, Dave Panciera, and Carrie Waters. "Evaluation of Dietary and Environmental Risk Factors for Hyperthyroidism in Cats." *Small Animal Clinical Endocrinology* 11, no. 2 (2001): 7.

10. J. Olczak, B. R. Jones, D. U. Pfeiffer, et al. "Multivariate Analysis of Risk Factors for Feline Hyperthyroidism in New Zealand." *New Zealand Vet Journal* 53, no. 1 (2005): 53–58.

CHAPTER 7

1. James E. Childs, Lesley Colby, John W. Krebs, et al. "Surveillance and Spatiotemporal Associations of Rabies in Rodents and Lagomorphs in the United States, 1985–1994." *Journal of Wildlife Diseases* 33, no. 1 (1997): 20–27.

CHAPTER 8

1. Valentina Merola and Eric Dunayer. "The 10 Most Common Toxicoses in Cats." *Veterinary Medicine,* 2006: 339–342, accessed at www.aspca.org/site/DocServer/vetmo606_339-342.pdf?docID=9643.

2. Animal Poison Control Center. "17 Common Poisonous Plants," accessed at www.aspca.org/site/PageServer?pagename=pro_apcc_common.

3. Valentina Merola and Eric Dunayer. "The 10 Most Common Toxicoses in Cats."

CHAPTER 9

1. D. C. Blood and V. P. Studdert. *Baillière's Comprehensive Veterinary Dictionary* (Oxford: Baillière Tindall, W. B. Saunders, 1988).

2. Beth Overley, Frances S. Shofer, Michael H. Goldschmidt, et al. "Association Between Ovariohysterectomy and Feline Mammary Carcinoma." *Journal of Veterinary Internal Medicine* 19, no. 4 (2005): 560–563.

3. www.isaronline.org/index.html.

4. www.dpd.cdc.gov/dpdx/HTML/Toxoplasmosis.htm.

5. www.petsandparasites.com/cat-owners/toxoplasmosis.html, www.pawssf.org, www.cdc.gov/healthypets, www.avma.org/animal _health/brochures/toxoplasmosis/toxoplasmosis_brochure.asp and www.cdc.gov/toxoplasmosis/pdfs/toxocatowners_8.2004.pdf.

CHAPTER 10

1. Carin A. Smith. "The Gender Shift in Veterinary Medicine: Cause and Effect." *Veterinary Clinics of North America: Small Animal Practice* 36, no. 2 (2006): 329–339. Veterinary Market Statistics, American Veterinary Medical Association, 2007, accessed at www.avma.org/reference/marketstats/usvets.asp.

2. American Association of Feline Practitioners Feline Vaccine Advisory Panel Report. *Journal of the American Veterinary Medical Association* 229, no. 9 (2006): 1405–1441, accessed at www .aafponline.org/resources/guidelines/2006_Vaccination_Guide lines_JAVMA.pdf.

3. E. C. Burgess. "Experimentally Induced Infection of Cats with Borrelia Burgdorferi." *American Journal of Veterinary Research* 53, no. 9 (1992): 1507–1511.

4. Veterinary Market Statistics, American Veterinary Medical Association, 2007, accessed at www.avma.org/reference/marketstats/usvets.asp.

5. D. T. Crowe. "Cardiopulmonary Resuscitation in the Dog: A Review and Proposed New Guidelines (Part II)." *Seminars in Veterinary Medicine and Surgery (Small Animal)* 3, no. 4 (1988): 328–348. B. A. Gilroy, B. J. Dunlop, H. M. Shapiro. "Outcome from Cardiopulmonary Resuscitation in Cats: Laboratory and Clinical Experience." *Journal of the American Animal Hospital Association* 23, no. 2 (1987): 133–139. W. E. Wingfield and D. R. Van Pelt. "Respiratory and Cardiopulmonary Arrest in Dogs and Cats: 265 cases (1986–1991)." *Journal of the American Veterinary Medical Association* 200, no. 12 (1992): 1993–1996. Philip H. Kass and S. C. Haskins. "Survival Following Cardiopulmonary Resuscitation in Dogs and Cats." *Journal of Veterinary Emergency Critical Care* 2, no. 2 (1992): 57–65.

6. Atul Gawande. *Complications: A Young Surgeon's Notes on the Imperfect Science* (New York: Metropolitan Books, 2002). E. C. Burton and P. N. Nemetz. "Medical Error and Outcome Measures:

Where Have All the Autopsies Gone?" *Medscape General Medicine* 2, no. 2 (2000). G. D. Lundberg. "Low-Tech Autopsies in the Era of High-Tech Medicine: Continued Value for Quality Assurance and Patient Safety." *Journal of the American Medical Association* 280, no. 14 (1998): 1273–74.

7. American Veterinary Medical Association: "What You Should Know About Choosing a Veterinarian for Your Pet." June 2004, accessed at www.avma.org/animal_health/brochures/choosing_vet/choosing_vet_brochure.asp.

8. Karen Allen, Barbara E. Shykoff, and Joseph L. Izzo. "Pet Ownership, But Not ACE Inhibitor Therapy, Blunts Home Blood Pressure Responses to Mental Stress." *Hypertension* 38 (2001): 815–820.

RESOURCES

AGE COMPARISON CHARTS:
- *www.antechdiagnostics.com/petOwners/wellnessExams/howOld.htm*
- *www.idexx.com/animalhealth/education/diagnosticedge/200509.pdf*

AMERICAN COLLEGE OF VETERINARY BEHAVIORISTS:
- *www.dacvb.org*

AMERICAN COLLEGE OF VETERINARY EMERGENCY AND CRITICAL CARE:
- *www.acvecc.org*

AMERICAN COLLEGE OF VETERINARY NUTRITION:
- *www.acvn.org*

AMERICAN VETERINARY DENTAL COLLEGE:
- *www.avdc.org/index.html*

AMERICAN VETERINARY MEDICAL ASSOCIATION:
- *www.avma.org/*
- *www.avma.org/reference/marketstats/default.asp*
- *www.avma.org/reference/marketstats/vetspec.asp*

AMERICAN SOCIETY FOR THE PREVENTION OF CRUELTY TO ANIMALS:
- *www.aspca.org/site/PageServer*
- *www.aspca.org*

BANFIELD, THE PET HOSPITAL:
www.banfield.net

CAT FANCIERS' ASSOCIATION:
- *www.cfa.org*

CAT FENCE:
- *www.purrfectfence.com*

COMPANION ANIMAL PARASITE COUNCIL:
- *www.capcvet.org*
- *www.petsandparasites.com*

CENTERS FOR DISEASE CONTROL AND PREVENTION:
- *www.cdc.gov/healthypets*

CORNELL FELINE HEALTH CENTER:
- *www.vet.cornell.edu/FHC*

CREMATION JEWELRY:
- *www.ashestoashes.com*
- *www.memorypendants.huffmanstudios.com*

EUKANUBA/IAMS CAT FOOD COMPANY:
- *www.us.eukanuba.com/eukanuba/en_US/jsp/Euk_Page.jsp?pageID=OT*

INTERNATIONAL SOCIETY FOR ANIMAL RIGHTS:
- *www.isaronline.org/index.html*

MERIAL FRONTLINE AND HEARTWORM PRODUCTS:
- *www.merial.com*

PETSHOTEL:
- *www.petshotel.petsmart.com/*

PET SUPPORT HOTLINE:

- *www.vet.cornell.edu/Org/PetLoss*
- *www.vet.cornell.edu/Org/PetLoss/OtherHotlines.htm*

POINT REYES BIRD OBSERVATORY:

- *www.prbo.org/*

POISON CONTROL HOTLINES:

- *www.petpoisonhelpline.com*
- *www.aspca.org/apcc*

PURINA:

- *www.purina.com/cats/health/BodyCondition.aspx*

SOFTPAWS:

- *www.softpaws.com/*

TOILET TRAINING:

- *www.karawynn.net/mishacat/toilet.html*
- *www.petplace.com/cats/how-to-toilet-train-your-cat/page1.aspx*
- *www.citikitty.com*

VETERINARY PET INSURANCE:

- *www.petinsurance.com/*

WELACTIN OMEGA FATTY ACIDS:

- *www.nutramaxlabs.com/Brochures/Welactin%20for%20Cats%20brochure.pdf*

ACKNOWLEDGMENTS

To my parents, whose wisdom I cherish—thank you for always believing in me and helping me follow my dreams. I don't know what I'd do without you. I love you both dearly.

To Dan—for learning to *like* my cats, and seeing this through to fruition. Once again, words can't express the gratitude for helping me survive it all.

It's a Dog's Life . . . but It's Your Carpet and *It's a Cat's World . . . You Just Live in It* would not have been possible without the wonderful support of Rick Broadhead, my literary agent; Heather Proulx, my editor; Alice Peisch, my publicist; and *everyone* else at Crown—a huge thank-you for taking this on!

And finally, to all the devoted animal lovers out there: whether it's been your random act of kindness of adopting that stray pet, or fostering one, or advocating ways of reducing pet overpopulation, or saving animal lives . . . thank you.

INDEX

fibrosarcomas, 153, 200, 201
fighting, 25, 64, 79
FIP (feline infectious peritonitis), 152, 153
FIV (feline immunodeficiency virus), 63–64, 152, 153
  testing for, 64, 162, 202–3
  in zoo cats, 190–91
flea preventatives, 76, 84–86, 205
  toxicities and, 85, 149, 162, 164, 165
fleas, 82, 209
  diseases transmitted by, 204, 205
flowers, toxic, 165
FLUTD (feline lower urinary tract disease), 17, 71–72
food, 76, 134–50. See also canned food; dry food
  "air burying," 150
  air travel and, 82, 83
  antisocial cats and, 128
  begging for, in early morning, 112
  binge eating and, 142
  contaminated, 134–35, 145–46
  exercising cat and, 131
  fiber content of, 69, 98, 142
  hair balls and, 69
  high-fiber, low-calorie, low-fat diet and, 137, 139
  high-protein diet and, 139–40
  homemade diet, 135, 142–43, 146–47
  milk, 141
  people, as treats, 147–48
  raw diet, 146
  reducing, for weight loss, 137
  starving picky eater until he eats and, 144
  top brands of, 145
  vegetarianism and, 142–43
Food and Drug Administration (FDA), 134–35
FORLs (feline oral resorptive lesions), 7
fostering cats, 189, 200
fraternal twins, 192–93
friendliness:
  genetics and, 19, 21, 127
  training and, 127–28
Frontline, 85, 173
FUO (feline urethral obstruction), 71, 92, 180–81, 187

furniture. See also scratching on furniture
  flea infestations and, 85
  rubbing face and body on, 106, 121

G
gardening, toxoplasmosis risk and, 193
genetics:
  coat color and, 18–20, 66
  deafness and, 66
  friendliness and, 19, 21, 127
  identical vs. fraternal twins and, 192–93
  inbreeding and, 189–90
  inherited diseases and, 37, 46, 77
  vigor of mutts vs. purebred cats and, 45
  wool sucking and, 97
Geological Survey, U.S., 93
glow jewelry and sticks, 164, 175
glutathione, 85, 171–72
goddesses, catlike, 87
grapes, 147–48
grass:
  cat, 152, 169
  eating, 141
gray long-haired cats, 21, 127
Gregory IX, Pope, 87
grooming, 51, 150
  brushing, 12, 36–37, 84
  cats too fat for, 138, 140
  hair balls and, 69
  licking "down there" and, 70–71
  of long- vs. short-haired cats, 36–37
  mat removal, 84
  shaving, 11, 12, 37, 84
guests. See houseguests

H
hair. See also color of coat; grooming
  dyeing, 78
  human, cat chewing on, 150
  shedding of, 10–13
  short- vs. long-haired cats and, 36–37
hair balls, 36, 37, 68, 69–70, 84
harness training, 124
health benefits of cat ownership, 224
health certificates, 82
heartworm disease, 205–6
heat (estrus), 177–78, 183–84, 192

ABOUT THE AUTHOR

DR. JUSTINE LEE is a board-certified emergency and critical care veterinary specialist and is the associate director of Veterinary Services at Pet Poison Helpline, a division of SafetyCall International. Previously, she was on the faculty at the University of Minnesota College of Veterinary Medicine. Dr. Lee graduated from Virginia Tech with a BS in Animal Sciences and then obtained her veterinary degree at Cornell University. She pursued her internship at Angell Memorial Animal Hospital, which is affiliated with the Massachusetts Society for the Prevention of Cruelty to Animals. In addition, she has completed an emergency fellowship and residency at the University of Pennsylvania. Currently, she is 1 of approximately 240 board-certified veterinary specialists worldwide in emergency and critical care and is a diplomate of the American College of Veterinary Emergency and Critical Care.

Dr. Lee has been published in numerous veterinary journals, including the *Journal of American Veterinary Medical Association*, the *Journal of Veterinary Emergency Critical Care*, and the *Journal of Veterinary Internal Medicine*. She has also published several veterinary book chapters, and has been aired on radio and television to promote preventative medicine, animal health, and the overall well-being of pets. Dr. Lee is a contributing author for *Prevention* magazine and various other breed newsletters. She lectures throughout the world on emergency and critical care.

When Dr. Lee is not working in the ER, she is playing

Ultimate Frisbee or ice hockey, hiking with her dog, traveling, or reading. Dr. Lee's three kids include:

- A rescued pit bull terrier (abandoned with parvovirus) named JP, for Jamaica Plain, where Dr. Lee worked in Boston

- A rescued gray and white tabby (abandoned with head trauma) named Seamus, for a former Irish-Bostonian-owned patient

- A rescued black cat (adopted after being diagnosed with a congenital heart defect) named Echo, from "echocardiogram," an ultrasound technique for the heart.